Ted Russell took this Paris scene with a hand-held 1000F, Tri-X film; 1/10, f/2.8, allowing the background to go black.

*les
barry*

HASSELBLAD

universal

photography

photo books

new
york

Preface

Since we can assume that the owner or prospective owner of a Hassel-blad camera has advanced beyond the very beginnings of photography, this book is not, as are so many camera guides, a course in the basic principles of photography in general. It is, instead, a discussion of two specific and individual camera systems — the unique 2¼ by 2¼ single-lens reflex system conceived and manufactured in Goteborg, Sweden, by Victor Hasselblad and the company that bears his name, and the equally unique (if not as well known) Hasselblad Superwides, eye-level cameras that give an almost incredible angle of view on 120-size film.

It is hoped that this book will serve to assist the present Hasselblad owner to derive an increased amount of enjoyment and service from his camera, and that it will help the potential owner to make up his mind, if doubt exists, as to whether or not to buy a Hasselblad.

Les Barry

The author gratefully acknowledges the contributions of so many photographers whose works are illustrated in this book, and who, thereby, contributed so greatly to making it possible. Special thanks are due Fred Onderka of Paillard Incorporated, a long-time and international associate of the author, for taking many of the technical photographs used here; and a vote of appreciation is offered Osten Wejerfelt of Victor Hasselblad AB for his contribution.

And for their tolerance during the completion of this project, thanks to Bruce Downes, editor and publisher of *Popular Photography Magazine;* as well as my wife, Frances, to whom this book is respectfully dedicated.

Contents

Ted Russell
Hasselblad 1000F, 135mm Sonnar, 1/100, f/11, Verichrome Pan film.

the

CAMERAS

ince its introduction on the market in 1948, the Hasselblad single-lens reflex system has undergone two modifications, or a total history of three models. The models have been designated the Hasselblad 1600F, the Hasselblad 1000F, and the Hasselblad 500C. These numerical designations refer directly to the specific shutter peculiarities of the individual models. The letter *F* stands for *focal plane*. The letter *C* means *Compur*. The actual numbers refer directly to the maximum shutter speeds of the models they identify — 1/1600 sec; 1/1000 sec, and 1/500 sec. Contrary to what one might expect, the course of the Hasselblad's development has been marked by a decrease of this maximum, the fastest having been the first model, and the slowest being the most recent. There are two reasons behind this reversal. The drop from 1/1600 sec to 1/1000 sec was aimed at greater efficiency and reliability, coupled with the realization that most photographers had little, if any, use for shutter speeds faster than 1/1000 sec. The drop from 1/1000 sec to 1/500 sec resulted from the change in type of shutter, viz., the discontinuance of the focal plane shutter with its safe maximum speed of 1/1000 sec in favor of the Compur shutter with its safe maximum speed of 1/500 sec.

To all intents and purposes, the only difference between the 1000F

George Holton
Hasselblad Superwide.

and 1600F lies in the difference in their respective maximum shutter speeds. For this reason we can discuss both cameras here as a single model. For purposes of identification, let's refer to this combined model as the Hasselblad-F, or focal-plane model. It was introduced shortly after the end of World War II, at a time when there was little radical activity in the field of 120-size camera design. To say that it captured the imagination of both the amateur and professional camera world would be to put it mildly. The Hasselblad was announced as a camera that met the de-

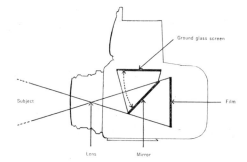

This diagram shows how the light entering the lens strikes the mirror between the lens and the film and is reflected upward to the focusing screen; or goes on to the film when the mirror is raised.

mands of photographers who wanted large-camera versatility in a 120 model, and, indeed, it fulfilled the claims made in its name.

Previous to the war the smallest format usually considered professional size was 4 by 5. The 4-by-5 press camera was the camera of the photojournalist. Professional film was cut film or film pack, and a mobile photographer was a strong-armed fellow who developed his muscles by lugging a heavy case full of equipment, holders, and film.

There was, it's true, a growing interest in the use of a roll-film camera for professional work, but those who did use them were looked on as a daring few. There were the 35mm devotees, whose work often delighted the salons, but whose photographs seldom were found published for editorial or advertising purposes. And there were the 2¼-by-2¼ *afficianadoes,* who used twin-lens reflex systems, and whose versatility depended almost solely on their ingenuity. Then, along came the Hasselblad, and an entire new area of photography was opened for the professional, as well as the advanced amateur.

Previously, many a professional who used a twin-lens reflex bemoaned the loss of three advantages of the large studio cameras — even though he was willing to bear with these shortcomings for the sake of the convenience of speed of operation, light weight, and film economy. He seriously felt the loss of lens interchangeability and the inability to change film type from shot to shot (although the Rolleiflex did provide an accessory cut-film back). He found the new problem of coping with parallax required him to waste too much of the precious small-film area in order to avoid cutting off important portions of his subjects.

These three failings were eliminated in one fell swoop by the Hasselblad system.

Because viewing is done through the taking lens, there is no parallax. A full line of accessory lenses was made available for this camera, from wide-angle through extreme telephoto. Film is loaded into a magazine which is completely detachable from the camera body, and which can be detached and replaced by another magazine containing a different type of film, at any point on the roll.

In addition, the Hasselblad reflex models feature a hood which can be removed and replaced by a special accessory hood for critical focusing.

safety features

The ingenious construction of this camera makes functional errors almost impossible. The film-advance knob also winds the shutter, thereby eliminating the danger of double exposures. A good practice in operating the camera is to advance the film and cock the shutter immediately after taking a picture. This will eliminate the possibility of removing a film magazine without the film's having been advanced and replacing it with one in which the film has been advanced. There exists, of course, the possibility of placing a magazine with the film already advanced on a camera with uncocked shutter or, the reverse, of putting on a magazine with film not advanced when the shutter has been cocked. However, there is no danger of either of the functional errors one might expect occurring, if, immediatly after changing magazines, the photographer checks, with a glance, the film and shutter signals on the right side of the camera. These signals are white when the film has been advanced and the shutter is cocked, red when the film has been exposed and the shutter released. When magazines are changed, the signals show the condition of the individual magazines, and the shutter signal shows the condition of the shutter. If the shutter and magazine signals do not match, remove the magazine and change the state of the shutter to comply with the magazine. If the magazine signal is red, release the shutter, attach the magazine, and wind the film-advance knob to advance the film, and then cock the shutter and bring both white signals into view. If the magazine signal is white, but that for the shutter is red, wind the advance knob, which — without a magazine attached — will cock the shutter, and next attach the magazine. In either case, you'll then be ready to shoot.

Removing the magazine cannot expose the film to light, because a metal slide is inserted into a slot in front of the film, protecting it when the magazine is off the camera. If you forget to insert the slide before preparing to remove the magazine, there's no danger. The magazine won't come off. If, after attaching the magazine, you forget to remove the slide, there's no chance of wasting a shot or running a blank roll of film through the camera, because the shutter release won't work while the slide is in place.

Although it's impossible to make an accidental double exposure with the Hasselblad, an intentional double exposure is quite easily accomplished.

12

Charles Stern
Hasselblad 500C, 1/50, f/5.6, Tri-X film.

Simply remove the magazine before winding the film advance knob, then turn the knob, thereby cocking the shutter, and reattach the magazine. A second exposure can then be made on the same piece of film.

what they have in common

All Hasselblads, the F-models, the 500C, the Superwide and the Superwide C, have one thing in common — interchangeable backs, both for roll and cut film.

In addition to this, the F-cameras and the 500C share the interchangeability of tops, which is to say, viewing and focusing hoods. And these hoods also may be used on the Superwide.

We will start, therefore, by discussing these features.

Underexposing for the silhouette effects, Ted Russell used fastest shutter speeds and small apertures for these two shots; got great depth of field and stopped most action, as well.

2

the

CAMERA BACKS

*T*he Hasselblad roll-film back (or magazine) is one of the most unique and appealing features of this system. It means that, by carrying extra magazines, the photographer is carrying, in effect, extra cameras. One might be loaded with fast black and white film for available light or indoor pictures; one might be loaded with slow black-and-white film for outdoor or fine-grain shots; still another might be loaded with daylight color film; and yet another, with tungsten-type color film. The photographer can switch film as many times as he chooses during a shooting session, to change emulsion or to go from black and white to color, without having to remove a partially exposed roll.

There are three types of film backs for the Hasselblad — the Magazine-12, the Magazine-16, and the cut-film adapter, which, of course, requires the addition of cut-film holders.

The Magazine-12, as its name indicates, gives twelve exposures on a roll of 120 film. These exposures are 2¼ by 2¼ (6 by 6cm) and represent what has come to be considered the ideal 120-size roll-film picture dimensions when used with a normal lens of 75 to 80mm. (More on these dimensions later, in the section on cropping.)

The Magazine-16, a recent addition, gives sixteen exposures on a

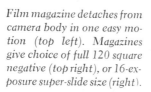

Film magazine detaches from camera body in one easy motion (top left). Magazines give choice of full 120 square negative (top right), or 16-exposure super-slide size (right).

roll of 120 film. These exposures are 1⅝ by 2¼ in. (4.5 by 6cm), and are most popular when used in conjunction with color film.

The Magazine-16 has caught on with professionals and amateurs for radically different reasons. Where the pro finds film to be the least of his expenses and is always willing to use more film than necessary to ensure getting *the* shot, the amateur considers economy of operation a major factor and is delighted to get four *extra* pictures per roll, particularly when it comes to the relatively expensive color films. The pro's interest in the Magazine-16, on the other hand, is this: He seldom uses a square picture, even though he prefers to make square negatives and have the freedom to crop in the printing. With color, though, and specifically with positive (reversal) color, the printing operation is eliminated, and any cropping must be done in the camera or as a mask on the finished transparency. With this in mind, he finds the 1⅝ by 2¼ size to be in his interest. This size, by the way, is a scaled-down version of the typical magazine-page dimensions.

Still a third magazine, the Magazine-16S, has been added to the Hasselblad line to accommodate the photographer who is interested in the more typical superslide size made popular by the small twin-lens reflexes, the 4 by 4's. The Magazine-16S gives sixteen exposures on a roll of 120 film, but these are cropped in the magazine to 1⅝ by 1⅝ (4.5 by 4.5 cm).

The Magazine-16 offers a couple of disadvantages which can be solved without too much difficulty. Though of very little importance

The cut-film adapter takes single sheet holders as shown above. The cutter, at right, is provided for cutting film to size.

to most photographers, when the dimensions of the picture are reduced, the effect on film is slightly telephoto with a normal lens.

The more important disadvantage of the Magazine-16 lies in the fact that its sixteen rectangular exposures are horizontal. Taking a vertical picture with a straight mirror reflex system is a little more than the average photographer can accomplish with equanimity. It can be overcome, though, by slipping the sportsfinder frame onto the *side* of the Hasselblad. The sportsfinder permits using the camera in its natural up-and-down position or on its side. But this can be awkward, because it means either that the camera must be focused through its reflex system and then turned on its side for sportsfinder viewing, or that focusing must be by guess or by zone.

A transparent plastic mask is dropped onto the ground glass when the Magazine-16 is being used. This mask is engraved to show both the 1⅝ by 2¼ area and the 1½ by 1½ area. Being transparent, it shows also the full 2¼ by 2¼ area, allowing the photographer to check the larger square and see if it would be more advantageous for the picture being taken. If he finds that it is, he can slip off the Magazine-16, replace it with the Magazine-12, and continue shooting. A black mask with a 1⅝ by 1⅝ opening is dropped on the ground glass to accommodate the Magazine-16S. Masks for both the Magazine-16 and the Magazine-16S also are available for use with the sportsfinder.

The cut-film adapter uses a 2½ by 2½ (6.5 by 9cm) sheet of film. However, since no film of this size is available on the market, a cutter is provided to slice the excess of a standard sheet of 2½ by 3½ film. The cutter is made of black-enameled steel over which has been installed a sheet of white plastic. The plastic serves to protect the film during the cutting, as well as permitting finger pressure to keep it in position. The rivets that hold the cover to the base serve also as a guide, stopping the inserted film at just the right point to keep a 2½ in. section inside the cutting edge.

17

Dean Vincent
Hasselblad 1000F, 135mm Sonnar, 1/100, f/8, Verichrome Pan film.

The adapter itself is attached to the camera body in much the same way as the roll-film magazines.

Of course, the film inserted into the cut-film adapter is enclosed in a cut-film holder. Each of the nickel-silver holders takes one sheet of film

The cut-film adapter enjoys safety devices similar to those of the roll-film magazine. Double exposures are prevented by a similar built-in catch that is tripped when an exposure is made. It prevents the camera's being recocked before the slide is inserted into the holder and the holder has been removed from the adapter. Intentional double exposures, though, can be made in the same manner as they are made with the magazine — by removing the holder, recocking the shutter, and reinserting the holder. Also, the cut-film adapter cannot be removed from the camera while a holder is in position, thereby eliminating the possibility of fogging the sheet of film.

What are the advantages of the cut-film adapter? Primarily, a much wider variety of cut films are made than are roll films. This means that many special-purpose photographs, involving individual technical problems that call for special films, can be solved by the use of cut film on the Hasselblad. Copying of various types of materials requires special films, as do police-laboratory and certain areas of scientific photography.

The availability of these special films frequently is unknown to the amateur photographer. How many of the following have you heard of?

(1) Ansco SSS Pan with a normal exposure index of 200* ASA for sports and portraiture.

(2) Ansco Commercial, a non-color-sensitive film, 25* ASA, for general copying.

(3) Ansco Commercial Ortho, 25* ASA, for copying blue prints.

(4) Du Pont Commercial, 24* ASA, non-color-sensitive.

(5) Du Pont Cronar High Speed Pan, 160* ASA, with a spectral response similar to that of the human eye, for portraits and other special work.

(6) Gevaert I-R Process, especially sensitive to infrared, for scientific and lab work.

(7) Kodak Contrast Process Pan, full color sensitivity, for copying color material.

This is just a sampling of the special films available only in sheets or plates. Plates may be used if the adapter's pressure plate is removed.

There are two other extremely important uses for cut film wtih the Hasselblad. One is when individual negatives require individual development. The other, for studio work, is when test exposures must be made and developed immediately. This is accomplished more readily (and economically) with single sheets of film.

loading the roll-film magazine

The roll-film magazine is made up of two sections, an inner section (the spool holder) and an outer shell. To load the magazine the spool holder must be removed from its shell. To do so, turn the spool-holder catch (on the left side of the camera when the lens is facing away from you) counter-

---

* Lesser ratings for use with tungsten.

Film loading is fast and simple. Remove spool holder (top left); insert film roll (top right); lock leader in place (center left); slip leader onto take-up spool (center right); insert holder into shell (bottom left); locking holder in shell releases film leader.

George Holton
Hasselblad 1000F, 1/5 (tripod), f/22, Panatomic-X film.

clockwise as far as it will go. Then, using the catch as a handle, pull the holder out of the shell.

When the holder has been removed, turn the catch clockwise. As you do, you'll notice two clamps, on either side of the film plane, open. Place the take-up spool in the top receptacle, the one which can be turned by a knurled knob protruding from the opposite (from the catch) side of the holder. Put the full roll of film in the opposite holder. The film should be loaded so that the end of its paper cover will (when the seal is broken) point downward, or away from the center of the holder. Next, break the seal and pull out about four inches of the paper. Pull the paper (black side should be facing you) across the film plane, sliding or tucking the outer edges under the two open clamps. Then, holding the paper in position, turn the catch counterclockwise again. This will lock the paper in the clamps. Now insert the end of the paper into the take-up spool and turn the knurled knob until the paper is tight. Slide the loaded spool holder back into the shell. When it is all the way in, turn the catch clockwise. This will release the paper clamps and lock the holder in.

Now open the film window on the back of the magazine. You should see the colored side of the paper. Then turn the loading key (opposite

21

George Holton
Hasselblad 1000F, 135mm Sonnar, exposure by meter, Verichrome Pan film.

side of the camera from the catch) clockwise until the number *1* appears in the little window. Turn the loading key backward, counterclockwise, as far as it will go. This will bring the *No. 1* into position in the automatic exposure-counter window. From here on, the film advance will be automatic.

The roll-film magazines may be loaded while on or off the camera. If the magazine is *on* the camera it is not necessary to have the slide in. However, if the magazine is *off* the camera you must be certain the slide is in place before you start loading.

The cover of the film window has a film indicator to remind you of the film type in each magazine. Some photographers prefer to stick a strip of masking or adhesive tape on the top of each magazine (particularly when more than just a couple are loaded and ready for use), identifying the magazine's contents by writing on the tape.

After the twelfth exposure, the shutter release is automatically locked. However, you can turn the film-advance knob one more time in order to cock the shutter and bring the white signal up in the magazine window.

To remove a magazine, place the camera in your left hand, with the lens pointing away from you. Press the magazine catch (the button on top of the magazine) to the right with your right thumb. The magazine will flop off into your right hand.

To attach a magazine, engage the hooks at the bottom of the camera to the bottom of the magazine. Push the magazine against the camera body. Slide the catch to the right to engage the top lock, and then slide it to the left.

tips on using the roll-film magazine

Remove the slide immediately after attaching a magazine. This will save time when you're ready to shoot.

When the slide is in position, its curled side should always point toward the front of the camera body (facilitates loading).

Always keep the slide at right angles when removing or inserting it (prevents the development of light leaks, or damage to the gasket that holds it in place).

Remember, you can't remove the magazine when the slide is removed. You can't operate the camera when the slide is in.

If you plan to take a lot of pictures, load as many magazines as possible with the same type of film (great time-saver).

Always make it a point to identify the contents of a magazine. However, if you should neglect to do so, it's possible to check by opening the film window and trying to identify the film by the color of its paper. If you should do so, do so in *very subdued* light.

You'll save time if you make sure that film and shutter signal windows are the same color before you attach a magazine.

3

the *VIEWING*
and *FOCUSING*
system

*b*ecause the Superwide and Superwide C are not reflex cameras and, therefore, have completely different viewing and focusing systems than the other, more popular models, we will not refer to them in this chapter or in other sections in which their functions do not coincide with those of the reflex models. Instead, we will discuss the Superwides individually in a separate section.

Both the Hasselblad F-cameras and the 500C use the basic form of mirror-reflex viewing and focusing. That is, the light reflected from the subject enters the lens and strikes a mirror which is placed, at a 45-degree angle, between the lens and the film plane. The light is then reflected upward and an image, the same as that which would appear on the film, is projected on a ground-glass screen. This image is focused by turning a knurled ring on the lens barrel. Since the mirror dissects (at 45 degrees) the 90-degree angle formed by the ground-glass screen and the film plane, the light reflected from the mirror travels the exact same distance from the mirror position to the ground glass as from the mirror position to the film plane. Therefore, when an image is in focus on the ground-glass screen, it will be in focus on the film when the mirror, by the action

George Holton
Hasselblad Superwide.

Ted Russell
Hasselblad 1000F, 60mm Distagon, 1/10, f/5.6, Tri-X film.

of the shutter release, is raised out of the way to allow the light to travel from the lens directly to the film.

Hasselblads boast an especially bright viewing and focusing image for two reasons. The ground glass itself is so extremely fine as to be almost grainless. The brightness of the image is increased and evenly distributed over the entire ground-glass area, even to the corners, by the addition of a Fresnel lens.

freedom from parallax

The fact that a delay must take place between the time the shutter is released and actually goes off is considered a slight disadvantage in single-lens reflex photography. However, most single-lens reflex fans consider

The Magnifying Hood, adjustable for individual eye-sight, slips on in place of the regular focusing hood; keeps out extraneous light and allows 2½ power critical focusing. It covers the entire picture area.

this more than offset by the fact that parallax is eliminated from the system.

Parallax is the slight difference between what you see through the viewfinder or viewing lens of other types of cameras and what registers on the film. This problem cannot be completely eliminated from other types because the taking lens and the viewer are, in spite of any amount of correction, looking at the subject from different angles. It is considered a particular inconvenience in close-ups, when the angle is sharply increased. Photographers concerned with very careful composition, especially when using positive color film — which does not have the black and white's darkroom cropping advantages — consider parallax a frequent nuisance.

Since the single-lens reflex user views through the same lens that does the taking, there is no difference in the angle of view. Hence, no parallax.

the focusing hoods

The collapsible focusing hood that comes with the camera is opened by sliding its locking catch to the right. This catch is located at the back of the hood, directly in front of the film-magazine catch. The hood is spring-mounted, and will snap up into position for its primary purpose — shading the ground-glass screen.

Just inside the top of the hood is a magnifier. This is released by pressing the same catch (that released the hood) further to the right. The magnifier, which is focused on the ground glass, is a very convenient aid to focusing, but is of special convenience when focusing on a poorly lighted subject.

27

George Holton
Hasselblad 1000F, 1/5, f/22, Panatomic-X film.

Before closing the hood, the magnifier must be returned to its closed position. To close the hood, fold the sides over the ground-glass screen, push the back forward, and then pull the front down.

The hood is easily removed to facilitate cleaning the ground glass, or for switching to the magnifying hood.

The magnifying hood is of most value when taking pictures in very dim or very bright light. In dim light, it permits the finest focusing, because of its high degree of magnification. In bright light, it cuts out all

George Holton
Hasselblad 1000F, exposure by meter, Panatomic-X film.

extraneous light which might interfere with the most efficient use of the ground glass.

The magnifying hood is made of aluminum and stainless steel, and is topped with a turnable soft rubber eyepiece. The coated magnifying lens allows 2½ power magnification for a 100mm focal length. It is adjustable for individual eyesight by turning a focusing ring located just under the eyepiece. This allows a change in diopter rating to any point from − 3 to + 3.5.

29

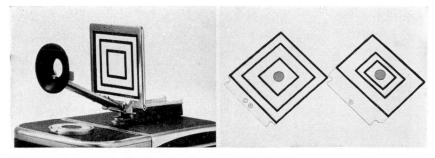

With the camera turned on its side, the sports finder is in its most convenient position for shooting. Transparent masks are supplied for all magazines; masks are ruled for use with accessory lenses.

To install this accessory, remove the regular focusing hood (after taking off the magazine) by sliding it to the rear of the camera. Install the magnifying hood by sliding it forward in the grooves vacated by the other hood.

Always fold the focusing hood before removing it.

the sports viewfinder

The Hasselblad sports viewfinder is an accessory that fits on a bracket on the left side of the camera. It's a double-frame finder, and is parallax-corrected by sliding the rear sight along a graduated scale. The finder folds flat, so as to be out of the way when not in use. It is adapted to telephoto lenses by the addition of blue lucite masks which fit in the grooves on the front frame.

The finder also can be masked to accommodate the Magazine-16.

Built into the base of the Hasselblad-F-type sportsfinder are contacts for both flash and strobe. This is necessary because both the sportsfinder and the regular flash shoe use the same mounting bracket, connecting with the camera's built-in synchronization. Flash contacts are not used on the 500C's sportsfinder, since this model's synchronization is built into the lens barrel and does not coincide with the sportsfinder.

The most convenient shooting position with the sports viewfinder seems to be with it on top of the camera; this is accomplished by turning the camera on its side. The position is easily changed, though, giving a choice between vertical and horizontal format when the Magazine-16 is being used.

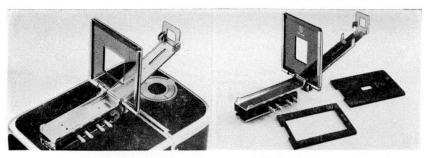

Sports viewfinder for the 1000F has flash and strobe contacts built-in. Individual masks are supplied for use with accessory lenses.

the prism sports viewfinder

The prism sports viewfinder combines the single-lens-reflex system's through-the-lens focusing with the frame-type fast-action sports viewfinder. This finder slides onto the top of the camera, over the ground-glass screen, in place of the regular viewing and focusing hood. The photographer follows the action through the frame as he does with other sports finders. However, without changing the position of the camera he can glance down through the prism to check focus and depth of field on the ground glass.

The tube through which he sees the ground glass also carries the eyepiece of the sports finder. This tube is easily shortened and lengthened, by turning a knurled knob on its side, and allows the photographer to correct the sports finder for parallax. A distance scale, for this purpose, is engraved on the tube in both feet and meters.

The masks are engraved for 80, 150, and 250mm lenses. A separate mask, for the 16-exposure magazines, may be used instead of the square mask. Each mask has a polarizing center point.

the penta-prism viewfinder

The penta-prism viewfinder, a late 1960 addition to Hasselblad viewing and focusing, makes possible eye-level viewing and focusing of an unreversed image seen through the lens. The penta-prism housing slides onto the top of the camera in the same manner as do the regular and magnifying hoods. It contains a five-sided prism that reverses the backwards ground glass image and projects it to the eyepiece.

4

the

F-CAMERAS

*C*ould the recent history of camera development be broken down into categorical periods, it is more than likely that there would be three major ones. Loosely speaking, these would be marked by general technical development; interchangeability; and, finally, automation. When the first Hasselblads, the F-Cameras, were introduced, the first stage in photography's history had already taken place. Technical development had been refined to a degree that must have been far beyond the wildest dreams of Niepce, Daguerre, Talbot, and the other fathers of photography.

The second stage, interchangeability, had already made great progress toward perfection in both the large and miniature camera fields, but apparently it was stymied — either for lack of interest or lack of direction — in the case of the medium-size roll-film camera. With one fell swoop, Victor Hasselblad gave the medium-size camera so full a measure of interchangeability that his contribution was the instant rival of the large and miniature cameras. It was this interchangeability, in both front and rear, that brought the earliest Hasselblads to the attention of every level of photographer, amateur and professional. It was the fact this inter-changeability was featured on a 120-size camera that provided the addi-

James M. Zanutto
Hasselblad 1000F, 1/500, f/8, Verichrome Pan film.

From the Hasselblad 1600F to the . . .

tional convenience of a reflex system, moreover, a *single-lens* reflex system, which meant the end of parallax — that made the Hasselblad worthy of special attention.

Even though a simple system, the first Hasselblad cameras were considered automatic to the extent that pressing the shutter-release button released the shutter, after automatically flipping the viewing mirror up and out of the way. Winding the shutter, then, advanced the film and automatically brought the mirror back into position for viewing and focusing. The Hasselblad F-cameras were considered as being based on a simple reflex system in that light reflecting from the subject entered the lens, which directed it to a mirror, which bounced it up to a ground-glass viewing screen, where the subject was seen right-side-up, but backward.

Focusing the F-camera is done by turning a knurled focusing ring on the lens barrel. For the greatest visibility and accuracy, this is done with the diaphragm of the lens all the way open.

lenses

Lenses for the F-cameras are of the preselection type. This means that an aperture may be selected previous to focusing and viewing. The

... *Hasselblad 500C there's little change in basic silhouette.*

camera is then focused with the lens open, and then, without removing his eye from the viewing position, the photographer can manually stop down the lens to his preselected aperture. In order to make this possible, two additional rings on the lens barrel are used. The preselector ring has no effect on the actual aperture. It is turned until the red mark on it points to the desired *f*-stop. Then the camera is focused. After focusing, the photographer flips the small handle on the actual aperture ring, turning the ring as far as it will go. It will not go beyond the desired *f*-opening, because the coupling of the preselector ring stops it. For speed of operation, use your right thumb and middle finger to operate the focusing ring. Keep your right forefinger on the handle (trigger) of the preselector ring. Then, immediately after focusing, slide the trigger to the right and up. It's a good habit to slide the trigger all the way to the left again immediately after focusing, in order to be prepared for the next shot.

A quick way to check and make sure the lens has been stopped down is to glance at the red marking on the two rings. If the red triangle on the preselector ring is opposite the red dot on the aperture ring, the camera is ready.

With the non-automatic F-Cameras, this lever is flipped as far as it will go, diaphragm stops at pre-selected aperture.

depth of field

Each lens is engraved with a depth-of-field scale. In order to control depth of field in operating the camera, it is recommended that you first focus on the nearest object to be included in the picture, learning, thereby, its exact distance from the film plane. Then, focus on the farthest object in the picture, determining its distance. If these two points lie outside the scale indicated for the f-stop you plan to use, it is necessary to stop down further, compensating by substituting a slower shutter speed. Or, if more is in focus than you prefer to have sharp within the picture, you can adjust by either opening the diaphragm or manipulating the focusing ring to throw out of focus the foreground or background area you prefer to have unsharp. Many professional photographers, who are interested in the most exact depth of field, use still a different method. They find it more to their preference to actually close down the aperture ring to the shooting f-stop and view through the reduced aperture. Since they are viewing through the taking lens, they are able actually to see the exact depth of field of the proposed photograph. However, since less light is transmitted through the closed-down diaphragm, this makes seeing a bit of a strain, particularly at the smallest apertures.

The focal plane shutter of the Hasselblad F-cameras is unique in that it is made of steel — a climate-proof Swedish steel that's so thin (about 1/500 in.) as to be almost as flexible as cloth. Its speeds are 1 sec to 1/1600 or 1/1000, depending on the model, including B. The shutter is synchronized for flash at all speeds from 1/25 sec up. For strobe or electronic flash, the Hasselblad 1000F is synced at 1/25.

The 1000F has a full complement of accessory lenses: 60mm f/5.6 (top left); 135mm f/3.5 (top right); and 250mm f/5.6.

synchronization

When using flash bulbs, use only focal-plane-type bulbs. A synchronizer adjustment, a small dial on the left side of the camera, just under the sports-viewfinder bracket, must be used to adjust the shutter to the individual flash bulbs. No adjustment is needed for strobe. The dial is numbered from 1 to 5, and a guide for their use, according to the individual selection of bulb, is provided in the camera instruction booklet.

An important point to remember is that the camera has two synchronization systems, flash and strobe, and that an individual contact is provided for each. Check, after attaching the cord, that it is plugged into the proper system.

accessory lenses

In addition to the normal 80mm f/2.8 lens, four accessory lenses were made for the Hasselblad F-cameras. These are, 60mm f/5.6; 135mm f/3.5; 250mm f/5.6, and 508mm f/5.6.

The 60mm Carl Zeiss Distagon focuses down to about 18 in., makes a good standard wide-angle lens, and provides the shortest focal length possible for a true wide-angle lens in a system of this type. A wider angle is possible with the Hasselblad Superwide cameras, which are discussed in another chapter.

The 80mm Zeiss Tessar focuses down to 20 in., and has a built-in sunshade.

37

George Holton
Hasselblad 1000F, 60mm Distagon, exposure by meter, Verichrome Pan film.

Two 135mm lenses have been made for the Hasselblad. One is a Zeiss Sonnar, the other is a Kodak Ektar. Both focus down to 40 in., are priced the same, and seem to differ basically only in that the user is provided a choice.

The above-listed lenses are all preset.

The 250mm Zeiss Sonnar is a long lens that focuses down to 8 ft., is popular with sports and wildlife photographers, and is quite useful for unobtrusive candids.

The 508mm Dallmeyer Tele Dallon converts the camera to a virtual telescope; is best used with a tripod, gunstock, or grip; and covers distances previously considered impossible with a 2¼ by 2¼ camera. It makes a very successful photographic accessory for the outdoorsman who "hunts" with a camera.

The fronts of the Hasselblad F-camera lenses are threaded to take a filter adapter ring. A ring is included with each lens. However, the same filters can be used for the 60, 80, 135, and 250mm lenses.

filters

The Hasselblad filters are made of homogeneous glass. Each is mounted in a black enameled aluminum holder.

Following are the filter factors:

COLOR	CODE	FACTOR
Yellow	Y	1.5
Yellow-green	YG	2
Green	G	3
Orange	O	4
Red	R	6

In addition, Hasselblad also makes a haze filter (code: HZ) for cutting down ultraviolet dominance in color pictures. This has no filter factor.

The Hasselblad POLA filter for the F-cameras, has a filter factor of 2. This filter is mounted in the adapter ring thread, and can be rotated a full 360 degrees within its own mount.

Because of the critical sharpness of the Hasselblad lenses, it is often desirable to soften or diffuse an image being photographed, particularly in portraiture, or to add a touch of softness to bright, harsh daylight landscapes. For this purpose there is available a diffusion filter, made of high-quality clear glass which has been engraved with a series of concentric circles. The effect of this filter is readily observed on the ground-glass screen. Its effect, in portraiture, can eliminate the necessity for retouching lines that might show up on the final picture as sharp and unflattering.

5

the

SUPERWIDES

*t*he Hasselblad Superwide has been called "the big eye" of photography, and justifiably so. In appearance, the camera seems to be practically all lens. In performance, the Superwide has proven to take in more, insofar as angle of view is concerned, than even the human eye.

what is it?

The Superwide is a camera of extremely wide angle for its 120-film size. The lens, a 38mm Zeiss Biogon, takes in a 90-degree image angle, which is impressive, if not fantastic, when you consider the film size, and the fact that this camera can be operated like any hand-held eye-level camera and is not confined to tripod use.

why a separate camera?

Apparently, the Hasselblad people saw a need or desire for a lens of this wide an angle. To fix such a lens to the other models of the Hasselblad

---

George Holton
Hasselblad Superwide, 1/100, f/11, Verichrome Pan film.

41

The big eye of photography, the original Hasselblad Superwide.

would have been a physical impossibility. Because the focal length of the lens is so short, its rear element has to be especially close to the film plane. Therefore, if an interchangeable 38mm lens had been made for any of the reflex models of the Hasselblad, it would have been impossible for the mirror to rise — it would have been obstructed by the back of the lens and its proximity to the back of the camera. We are talking about a true wide-angle lens, and not a retrofocus, which has been used to solve this problem on some of the newer lenses for the 35mm single-lens reflex cameras.

Having had the 38mm lens developed by the Carl Zeiss Works, the Hasselblad folks had it coupled with a Compur shutter. This lens and shutter were fixed to a special short camera body. In other words, instead of confining themselves to lenses that fit the regular bodies of their cameras, the Hasselblad engineers designed a camera body to fit the lens they wanted.

Then, since the film plane did not have to assume any particular peculiarities to suit this special lens-shutter-body combination, the back of the camera was fashioned after the already existing Hasselblad line, making it possible to interchange other Hasselblad backs with the Superwide back.

The lens opens to $f/4.5$, and has click stops of $f/5.6$, $f/8$, $f/11$, $f/16$ and $f/22$, with no vignetting at any aperture.

The shutter has ten speeds: B, 1, 1/2, 1/5, 1/10, 1/25, 1/50, 1/100, 1/250 and 1/500. It is completely synchronized for flash and strobe.

42

The Superwide's versatility is illustrated by these two photographs by George Holton. The top shot was made for a steel company in Pennsylvania; the bottom photograph is the interior of a home in Japan.

As with the other Hasselblads, the Superwide features interchangeability of viewing devices. At left, the eye-level viewer is slipped on to its clip on the camera body. The photo at right shows how a ground-glass back can be mounted on the camera.

viewing and focusing

Viewing is accomplished through a detachable eye-level viewfinder. Built into the viewfinder mount is a special prism which directs the vision down to the top of the camera. Built into the top of the camera is a small circular spirit level. While viewing through the viewfinder, the photographer's eye can catch the prism, which will permit him to see the level at the same time as he sees the subject. In this manner he can control the camera's position while hand-holding it, avoiding tilting, which can cause disastrous distortion with a lens of such a wide angle.

The viewfinder slides onto a shoe on top of the camera. In a camera of this wide angle, there is little if any necessity for parallax compensation. However, parallax is controlled by the fact that the viewfinder takes in just a little less than the lens does. Therefore, there is always that margin against parallax problems at the very edge of the negative.

For perfectionists, or for persons who want absolute control over distortion and perspective with this camera, there is an accessory ground-glass back which allows it to be used as a studio view camera for viewing and focusing. With the camera on a tripod, the film magazine is removed, and the ground-glass back is slipped onto the camera in its place. The ground-glass back is grooved so that either the regular Hasselblad focusing hood or the magnifying hood may be attached. Of course, the back must be removed and the film replaced before the exposure is made.

Focusing the camera is done by means of a knurled ring on the rear of the lens barrel, which can be turned in the usual manner to focus down to 19½ in. There is no rangefinder or visual checking system for focusing the camera in normal use (other than the ground-glass back). However, the depth of field of this lens is so great that no such device is necessary. An approximation of the camera-to-subject distance at any aperture can be counted on to give reasonably accurate sharpness in any case.

44

More of the interchangeability of viewing devices is illustrated in these two photo-graphs. At left is a magnifying hood; at right, the regular Hasselblad reflex hood. Both of these are used in conjunction with the ground-glass back.

The depth-of-field scale is located on the top of the lens barrel — as are the shutter speed and aperture scales — and is readily visible.

As an example of the Superwide's extreme depth of field, at ƒ/22 you have everything in complete sharpness from 25½ in. to infinity.

operation and uses

In operation, the camera is focused; shutter speed is set by turning a knurled ring beside the shutter-speed scale; and the aperture is set by sliding a small pointer. The shutter is cocked by pushing a trigger which is among the controls grouped on top of the lens barrel.

The film is advanced by turning a large knob on the right side of the camera — the same as with the other Hasselblads. Like the other models, the Superwide has the same signal system for checking to see if the film has been advanced, etc.

Unintentional double exposure is impossible. Intentional double exposures can be made by removing the back and cocking the shutter.

On the left side of the lens barrel, just below the flash contact, are the letters M and X, and a small lever that can be slid from one to the other. The setting for regular flash is M. The setting for electronic flash is X.

A word of caution. Most flash reflectors do not have the 90 degree angle of the Superwide, and a hot spot will result from using a single direct flash. This is avoided by the use of multiple flash, or by bouncing the light from the single one in order to spread it over the area covered by the lens.

A unique button controls the operation of the self-timer mechanism. This, too, is located on top of the lens barrel, just forward from the aperture scale. This button actually operates a guard which stops the

45

The Hasselblad Superwide C looks like a combination of the familiar Superwide silhouette with the automatic lens barrel of the 500C, plus the 500C's rapid advance crank. Notice, too, the new top-of-the-camera shutter release.

shutter-cocking trigger and ends its movement when the shutter is cocked for a regular exposure. By pulling back on the button, the trigger may be moved past it. The self-timer is then set. It is activated by the shutter release.

The uses of the Superwide are somewhat varied. Because of its all-inclusiveness, it is naturally practical in situations in which the photographer cannot step back far enough to include his entire subject with a normal lens or a conventional wide-angle lens. Architectural photographers will find the Superwide to be useful for this reason. Because of its wide image angle, vertically as well as sideways, the Superwide will catch the tops of most buildings while held perfectly level. Since it is not, therefore, necessary to tilt this camera, the distortions found so frequently in architectural photography will not exist. If only a portion of an area is desired, the Superwide is accommodating here, too, in avoiding distortion, because of its square format. Everything is included; however, when the final print is made, only that section of the negative that is desired, top or bottom, is retained in the print. The effect is one of giving a camera angle which is not straight on, but which is, nevertheless, free of distortion. The Superwide's large image angle and extreme depth of field make it quite useful for police and news photographers. The photographer can approach a scene; point his camera in its general direction, without taking the trouble to view or focus accurately; and be fairly certain that what he wants will be included in the picture, and that it will be in focus.

Remember, there is no hard-and-fast rule that says the camera must be level. By tilting it, the Superwide user can get some interesting distortions and other creative effects.

The Hasselblad Superwide C

The newest member of the Hasselblad camera line is the Hasselblad Superwide C, which has been designed for more working convenience.

The lens, the 38mm Zeiss Biogon, is similar to that found on the previous model. Built into the lens barrel, along with full synchronization for M and X flash and strobe, plus a self-timer, is the automatic Exposure Value Scale as found on the 500C.

New on the Superwide C is a top-of-the-camera release button. Also added to this camera is the 500C-type base plate which can be used for quick coupling to the tripod, or for a flash bracket.

The rapid advance crank built onto the Superwide C is of the automatic variety, in that it cannot be turned more than one frame, and in that it cocks the shutter automatically.

6

the

500C

i f any fault was found with the Hasselblad system by the large number of F-camera owners, it was expressed in an annoyance over one factor — that the lens had to be stopped down, manually, after focusing, and before shooting. Even the most experienced users, it would seem, suffered an occasional slip in this regard and absent-mindedly suffered an accidental overexposure. This fault, in fact, also plagued the 35mm single-lens reflex manufacturers, who solved it in several ways. One solution was to add a lever to the lens barrel — a lever that came into contact with the shutter release. This lever's function was to close down the lens to a predetermined aperture. Pressing the lever, then, closed down the lens and tripped the shutter. Another method was an internal linkage between the shutter release and the lens' diaphragm, extending from the body of the camera into the lens barrel. This, too, closed the lens opening to a set stop before allowing the shutter to perform its function. Both of these methods showed up on focal-plane–shutter-type single-lens reflexes. A third system, introduced on Zeiss's Contaflex cameras, made use of an entirely different method. Instead of linking a shutter in the back of the camera body with a diaphragm up front, in the lens barrel, this system concerned itself with the Compur shutter,

Jules Alexander
Hasselblad 500C; studio, strobes.

The Hasselblad 500C, single-lens reflex with automatic diaphragm, Compur shutter, interchangeable lenses, while maintaining full Hasselblad interchangeability.

a between-the-lens type, which is located in close proximity to the diaphragm. The function of this arrangement, again, was to close down the lens and operate the shutter in one operation. Because both the shutter and the diaphragm are contained in the lens barrel, this system might seem to be the simplest of the three. Actually, it is more complex than one might think.

operation

First of all, the shutter, being in the lens barrel, must be open during the viewing and focusing. For this reason, an extra step had to be added to the shutter operation — the shutter had to be closed before it could open to expose the film. Secondly, special precautions had to be taken to prevent fogging the film during the time the shutter was open for viewing and focusing.

It was this system that Mr. Hasselblad decided to use to bring automation to his camera, and here's how he did it — while retaining interchangeability:

Each lens, of course, had to have its own built-in shutter. This shutter is open during focusing and viewing, so an *auxiliary* shutter, a barn-door-type light baffle, was added to the camera body for the specific purpose of protecting the film during the time the main shutter is open. (The back shutter, by the way, can be used as a main shutter when regular Hasselblad built-in-shutter lenses are not employed.) When the front shutter is open, the back shutter is closed. When the front shutter is released, and closes down, the back shutter opens to permit a photograph to be taken.

That, though, is not the entire process. Here's how it works (and this is the sequence of operation):

The photographer presses the shutter-release button; the shutter closes; the diaphragm closes to a preset position; the back shutter opens; the mirror goes up and out of the way; the front shutter opens and shuts and the picture is taken; and the back shutter closes. Then, when the photog-

Les Barry
Hasselblad 500C, 1/60, f/8, Panatomic-X film.

rapher winds the film-advance knob, he advances the film; brings the mirror down into viewing position; opens and cocks the front shutter; and opens the diaphragm.

The actual time-lapse between pressing the shutter release and the taking of the picture is about 1/25 sec. In ordinary use, this delay will not interfere to any appreciable extent with the capturing on film of the image scene on the ground glass. But suppose, as in sports or other candid photography, the photographer finds he cannot spare the 1/25 sec. Pro-

Hasselblad versatility is important to such photographers as Ben McCall whose work calls on him to be able to carry a full photographic line into such situations as this. With a 500C, a couple of extra backs and lenses and a Superwide in his gadget bag he's ready for most exigencies. The pictures shown on the next page are printed from full negatives. With his Hasselblad lens variety McCall is able to find a point at which he can stand, then select the lens that will give him the picture.

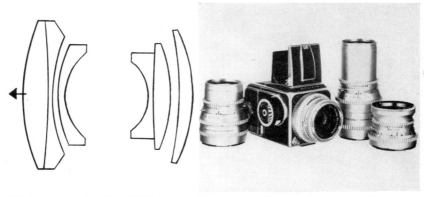

All five lenses for the 500C include Compur shutters and automatic diaphragms. Shown in the photograph with the camera are, left to right, 150mm Sonnar; 80mm Planar (on camera); 250mm Sonnar, and 60mm Distagon. (The 500mm Tele-Tessar is not shown.) The diagram shows the cross section of the 80mm Planar, the six element f/2.8 normal lens for the 500C.

vision is made for this eventuality. Right under the film winding knob is a small button, the quick-release button. By touching it, the photographer can set off all the normal operations that take place when the shutter release button is pressed, with the exception of actually operating the shutter, itself. In other words, the quick-release button will open the back baffle, raise the mirror, stop down the diaphragm, and close the shutter. Then, when he presses the shutter release the shutter will open and close immediately. In using this method, though, the photographer must use the sports viewfinder for viewing. Focusing has to be done in advance if the ground glass is required, or it may be performed by guessing the distance and adjusting the depth-of-field indicators to include the action being photographed.

Does all the foregoing mean that the Hasselblad 500C is a different camera from its forerunners in the Hasselblad line? The answer to that one is a hesitant "yes and no."

In the "no" department, there are these similarities: The 500C looks like its predecessors. In fact, all Hasselblad reflex cameras look enough alike to be almost indistinguishable to the uninitiated from a distance. The 500C enjoys the same interchangeability as did the earlier models. That is, lenses are completely interchangeable, backs are completely interchangeable, and focusing and viewing devices are completely interchangeable. The backs and tops are even interchangeable among the various models of the camera. The lenses of the 500C, though, do not fit the F-cameras, and vice versa — and herein lies the "yes" of the answer.

The normal lens for the Hasselblad 500C is a six-element 80mm Zeiss f/2.8 Planar. These elements are placed in the lens barrel in groups of three, with two elements in each group being cemented together.

54

Flash or strobe are bracketed to the camera on the tripod socket. Contact cord is plugged into the lens barrel contact. Selection for X or M is made on lens barrel next to contact. Flash can be used even with sports viewfinder on the camera.

Between these two three-element groups are the leaf-type Compur shutter, with speeds from B to 1/500 sec, and the diaphragm, with openings from $f/2.8$ to $f/22$.

This built-in shutter-diaphragm arrangement is found, also, on the four accessory lenses, a 60mm $f/5.6$ Zeiss Distagon, a 150mm $f/4$ Zeiss Sonnar, a 250mm $f/5.6$ Zeiss Sonnar, and a 500mm $f/8$ Zeiss Tele-Tessar.

A fourth accessory lens, a 250mm telephoto, was past the drawing board stage at the time this book went to press.

The use of the Synchro Compur shutter on the 500C, as opposed to the focal-plane shutters of the previous models, gives the Hasselblad a more workable flash-synchronization system. This system also is built into the lens barrel, and its contact is found on the left side of the barrel. Just below the flash contact is a lever under three markings, M, X and V. The M-synchronization is for use with all class M and S flash bulbs at all shutter speeds. When the lever is set at this control, the exposure is delayed to coincide with the peak of the bulb's intensity. The X-synchronization, for strobe and electronic flash at all speeds, works the other way around — it fires the high-speed flash when the shutter is fully open.

The V-setting is for the self-timer, which operates at all speeds except B. The self-timer setting is protected by a special safety device, a catch which is located just below the lever that designates the type of flash synchronization. Before the lever can be moved to V, the catch has to be pressed down. This prevents accidentally setting the camera on self-timing. The self-timer operates 8½ sec after it is set. When the shutter is released, the lever moves back to X. For this reason, the self-timer may be used with strobe.

The depth of field of the 60mm Distagon is illustrated in this Venetian scene by George Holton, with both extreme foreground and far background in focus.

exposure value system

In examining the shutter speeds and aperture ratings engraved on the lens barrels of the 500C's lenses, we find that the linear placement of these scales has been set up in an interesting manner. Whenever a combination of shutter speed and aperture rating is set, the number next to either (shutter or aperture) will be opposite a number of relative value. That is to see that the next shutter speed, if it's faster, will be opposite an aperture rating that is wider open to a compensating extent. For instance, if the camera is set for 1/125 sec at f/8, the 1/250 marking on the scale (rep-

56

Interchangeability of film advance knobs is illustrated here. Regular knob can be removed for accessory knob with built-in exposure meter, or accessory rapid advance crank.

resenting twice as much speed) will be opposite $f/5.6$ (twice as large an opening). Besides being neat, what does this mean? It means that the Hasselblad 500C's lenses have a built in Exposure Value System (EVS). This is a system of interlocking the two scales so that a change in one will result in a compensating change in the other. Furthermore, the EVS has a scale of numbers of its own. This will be found just to the right of the shutter-speed scale, just past $1/250$. It is the scale of numbers that begins with 2 and runs through 18.

It works in the following manner: The camera can be set either according to the desired combination of $f/$stop and shutter speed, or according to the EVS scale itself. In either case, the two scales are interlocked, and unless otherwise desired, a change in one will lead to a compensating change in the other. This is prevented in the same manner as is used to set the camera. By pushing the button located just on the camera side of the EVS scale, the photographer releases the coupling of the two exposure scales. He can then set the camera according to the desired aperture and speed — or he can reset the EVS number.

Each EVS number represents twice (or half, depending on the direction in which you're reading) the exposure value of the previous numbers. This scale may be set between numbers, too, if this is found to be necessary. The smallest numbers represent the least amount of light, and graduate upward.

The EVS number is found in one of two ways. Either the aperture and speed scales are set for the conditions under which the photograph is being made, setting the EVS pointer automatically on the correct EVS number; or the EVS number is determined by use of a meter or chart and set, automatically lining up the aperture and shutter combinations. Many exposure meters now give readings in EVS values as well as according to the conventional scales. Or there is a special Hasselblad meter which reads directly in EVS values.

This Hasselblad meter represents a further change in the system

Meter knob also can be worn on wrist with this accessory wrist band (left). Photo at right shows top view of lens barrel with its easy-to-read scales and convenient depth of field indicators.

as found in the 500C — interchangeable film-advance devices. In this case, the interchangeable knob which comes with the camera can be replaced by a knob with a built-in exposure meter. The meter, when installed, is on the right side of the camera, the same side as the EVS scale. Therefore, it becomes a simple matter to transfer the meter reading from the knob to the EVS scale without changing the camera's position. Because of its interchangeability, and therefore removeability, the meter can be used off the camera, as well. The meter can be used for direct reflected-light readings, or, by sliding the built-in translucent baffle over the exposed photoelectric cell, the user can employ his Hasselblad meter for incident-light readings.

An advantage of the EVS system is that it makes the computing of filter factors a simple and automatic process. If the filter factor is computed in the EVS number, which is then set accordingly, the compensation for filters becomes automatic.

depth of field

Also found on top of the lens barrel, just forward from the distance scale, are two windows, in each of which is a red pointer. These red pointers are the working members of the automatic depth-of-field scale. Since depth of field is determined by both distance and aperture, the position of these pointers is changed by a change in either the distance or aperture setting on the lens barrel. This is fully operative and completely accurate. When depth-of-field control is of special importance, it is achieved by first focusing on the nearest part of the object that is to be in focus and then focusing on the farthest point. These two distances, thus determined, will represent the maximum (or minimum, depending on the particular problem) depth of field necessary to a successful photograph.

The earliest lenses made for the 500C did not offer a method for manually stopping down the diaphragm in order to *see* the depth of field on the ground-glass screen. However, this has been changed, and now each 500C lens (all focal lengths) includes a manual diaphragm control. This control is visible in the form of a small lever on the lens barrel,

The small lever in the circle in the photo at left is the manual diaphragm control. By pushing it, the photographer releases the automatic diaphragm, which stops down for critical depth of field control while focusing. Photo at right shows the rear shutter, a baffle which protects the film between exposures, but which also may be used as a shutter when lenses without built-in shutters are attached to the 500C.

slightly to the rear of the highest numbers on the EVS scale. By pressing this lever, the photographer releases the diaphragm, which stops down, automatically, to any preset opening.

rear shutter

As mentioned, it is possible to use the rear shutter as a main shutter, though only on slow speeds, because this shutter is operated by what amounts to a direct drive between it and the shutter-release button. That is to say, the rear shutter stays open only for the length of time that the release is pressed. Removing the pressure from the release button allows the back shutter to swing shut. This is useful with auxiliary lenses which do not have the regular between-the-lens shutter of the standard 500C lenses. Also, the operation of the rear shutter is recommended when the camera is used for micro/macro photography with bellows extensions and special lenses.

Because the rear shutter remains open only when there is pressure on the button, the user must be careful, when using the regular automatic lenses, not to release the button before the shutter has gone off. This is particularly important with slow exposures. Releasing the button will close the back screen, cutting off exposure that has not been completed.

The shutter-release button is marked with two settings, T and O, and is controlled by a moveablelever. When the lever is at O, the camera is ready for instantaneous speeds. When the lever is moved to T, it locks the release button in its depressed position for time exposures. Swinging the lever back to O will release the button and end the exposure.

other extras

Quick-focusing handle attaches to a ring that fits on focusing ring of lens barrel. Model 1 fits 60 and 80mm lenses; model 2 fits 150 and 250 lenses.

The 500's base plate (top left) has European and American tripod screws, and couples to a quick-action tripod head (top right) for fast mounting onto or removal from tripod. Bottom left photo shows how Hasselblad filters slip onto inner bayonet ring, and can be used with sunshade, which (bottom right) slips onto outer bayonet.

The bottom of the camera is, first of all, threaded for both European and American tripods. In addition, the metal plate is such that it can be used with a quick-action tripod head. With this accessory, the camera can be slid on or off the tripod rapidly.

The electric motor, which will be available for the 500C, will be fastened to the front of the camera by means of the two mysterious holes on the front of the camera, just to the left of the lens barrel when you are facing the lens. This motor will be coupled to the bayonet mount of the interchangeable film-advance mechanism.

Another seemingly mysterious hole, just under the sports-viewfinder bracket, has been added to the camera to accommodate a tiny hook. The function of this hook is to hold the flash cord, keeping it from flopping in front of the lens, or otherwise inconveniencing operation.

Two sets of bayonet mounts are built into the front of each lens barrel. The inner mount is for filters and correction lenses. The outer mount holds the sunshade. All 500C lenses have the same size bayonet mounts, and accommodate filters interchangeably.

The advantages of single-lens reflex for the pictorialist are shown here. George Holton exposed at the precise moment for the picture he saw on his ground glass. Taken with an 80mm lens, 1/500, f/11, Verichrome Pan film.

7

using the

HASSELBLAD

*W*e commented (in Chapter 4) that, before the advent of the Hasselblad, the 120-size roll-film camera had reached a high point in technical development, and that, in 1948, Victor Hasselblad introduced interchangeability to this category of small camera. It was interchangeability, more than any other single factor, that made the introduction of the Hasselblad system a landmark in photographic history.

We also pointed out that there was a third major phase in the history of photography — the current one, *automation*. In December, 1957, Hasselblad made the big leap into automation when he introduced the 500C. Because a single push of the shutter-release button stops down the diaphragm, raises the mirror, and activates the shutter, this is an automatic camera. The question arises, is there anything about the automatic camera that requires that it be used in some manner other than that in which the nonautomatic camera is used? The answer to that question is this: An automatic single-lens reflex camera is operated like any non-single-lens reflex camera. This is not to include nonautomatic single-lens reflex cameras. It is the nonautomatic SLRs that require something extra — namely, the manual stopping down of the diaphragm. With the automatic

George Holton
Wide angle (Distagon) shot, underexposed for silhouette.

63

SLR the user sets the aperture scale before even viewing and focusing, and shoots as though the diaphragm were already adjusted to its taking position.

However, the user must keep one thing in mind. In the automatic single-lens reflex, the camera performs certain functions that the non-SLR does not perform. In the case of the Hasselblad 500C, these are the stopping down of the diaphragm, the raising of the mirror, the uncovering of the film plane and the closing, before opening, of the shutter. As mentioned, these functions take about 1/25 sec. Therefore, there is that much delay between the pressing of the release button and the actual taking of the picture, and this delay should be taken into consideration, especially when photographing moving objects.

viewing

The image, as seen on the ground glass of the Hasselblad, will appear right side up, but backward — the same as that which appears on the ground-glass screen of twin-lens reflex cameras. Viewing, for that reason, takes some getting used to. The natural tendency is to move the camera, when adjusting the view, in the direction of the subject as seen on the ground glass, and there is a certain amount of confusion, at first. When photographing a moving subject, you'll find, in the beginning, that you miss a lot of pictures because you've moved the camera in the wrong direction. The camera must be moved in the direction that the subject is moving in, in order to follow it, rather than in the direction it appears to be moving in on the ground-glass screen. The solution comes, of course, with practice. You must practice moving the camera in the direction opposite that in which the subject seems to be moving. It will seem perfectly reasonable, after a while.

Any camera in which the mirror must move upward and out of the way of the lens in a fraction of a second will be subject to a certain amount of vibration, as a result of this motion and its sudden stop. Therefore, it is more important with a single-lens reflex than with other cameras that it be held firmly while the exposure is being made. Fortunately, the Hasselblad was designed with a large, flat bottom, one which will accommodate a firm grip. The ideal way to hold the camera is as follows. Hold it in the palm of your left hand, grasping one side of its body with your thumb and the other side with your second, third, and fourth fingers. This leaves the index finger free to trigger the shutter release. Keep your left wrist pressed tightly against your chest. Since all other controls are either on the right side of the camera or in front, all other functions can be performed with your right hand. Use it for focusing, setting the exposure scales, and advancing the film. For the steadiest and quickest operation, leave your right hand on the lens barrel after focusing, using it as an

When using a Hasselblad, grip camera base with left hand, left forefinger ready to release shutter; focus with right hand.

extra support for the camera. Push the shutter release with your left index finger, but do so smoothly, being careful not to jar the camera.

Remember, the rear shutter is linked directly to the shutter-release button, and stays open only as long as the button is depressed. Do not, particularly on slow exposures, merely tap the button and release it. This can result in the back shutter's being partially or even completely closed again by the time the mirror is raised, the diaphragm is stopped down, and the front shutter closes and opens to make the exposure. This factor, of course, does not concern the user of the F-cameras or the Superwides. However, all photographers should take care to develop a technique for operation of the shutter release in a smooth and firm manner, so as to avoid camera shake at any shutter speed.

When using the camera at eye level, with the sports viewfinder, you will not have the advantage of the heavy grip at its base. In this case, press the camera firmly against your face. Operation is similar to that used when using the reflex finder. That is, use the left hand for gripping, the right hand for focusing, and the left index finger to release the shutter.

exposure meter and film

There is no disputing the value of an exposure meter in determining the proper aperture and shutter speed at which to take a particular picture. However, an improperly used meter can give a completely false reading, resulting in an under or overexposed picture. This danger of improper

George Holton
Telephoto shot made with 135mm lens, camera on tripod.

use is quite prevalent when the exposure meter is built into the camera. The danger arises from the natural tendency to use the meter from the camera position — particularly when the camera is on a tripod. Fortunately, the Hasselblad's meter is an interchangeable accessory, and can be removed from the camera at the flick of a button. Don't hesitate to take advantage of this convenience. You may be reluctant to hold a camera up close to a subject's face for a careful reflected light reading, or to place the camera in the subject's position for an incident light reading. Neither of these is necessary. Simply remove the meter from the camera and use it in the same fashion you would any meter. Take your reflected reading carefully, close to the area of medium exposure. Or, for special effects, take a direct reading in the shadow area if you want shadow detail in your picture; take it against the highlights if you want the highlights to have tone. Remember, though, that either of these extremes in exposure will result in extremes in the final print. If you take the reading off the shadow area, any highlights are going to be completely washed out. If you take the reading on the highlights, the dark areas are going to fall off into black. Some adjustment of these can be made in printing, with dodging or burning in, but the results will still be extreme.

The Hasselblad meter knob is supplied with a sliding white baffle which, when moved into position over the photoelectric cell, converts the meter to one that measures incident light. It works in the same manner as does any other incident-light-type meter. That is, it is placed in the subject's position, and aimed directly at the camera lens. Since the white baffle creates an artificial highlight that extends across the entire surface of the cell, it gives a constant measurement of the light falling on the subject.

It's true that most black-and-white film has a certain amount of "built-in" latitude, and that faulty exposures also can be corrected in the development as well as the printing. However, it's important that accurate readings be taken when using positive color film. In the first place, color film has practically no latitude, and there's little that can be done in development to compensate for a faulty exposure. And, of course, there's no chance to make up for it in the printing, since the film (the transparency) is the end product.

But besides giving you pictures that are lighter or darker than they should be, faulty exposure of color film also gives you incorrect color. Overexposure washes out colors, adding a slight blue cast to the picture; underexposure adds a red cast that distorts colors at that end of the scale.

As a bit of sidelight advice, the fact that over and underexposure does distort color is the basic reason for maintaining a slim color balance in your pictures. This is to say that the brightest area should not be more than twice as light as the darkest area when bright colors are involved, or more than three times as light when soft, warm colors are involved. Since it is impossible to balance the exposure of any greater range, a more severe balance will distort the colors at one end of the scale or other, if not both.

Most professionals, even though they use meters, are in the habit of bracketing their exposures. And this is particularly true with color. That is, they make three exposures for each shot — one slightly over and one slightly under the meter reading, just to be sure.

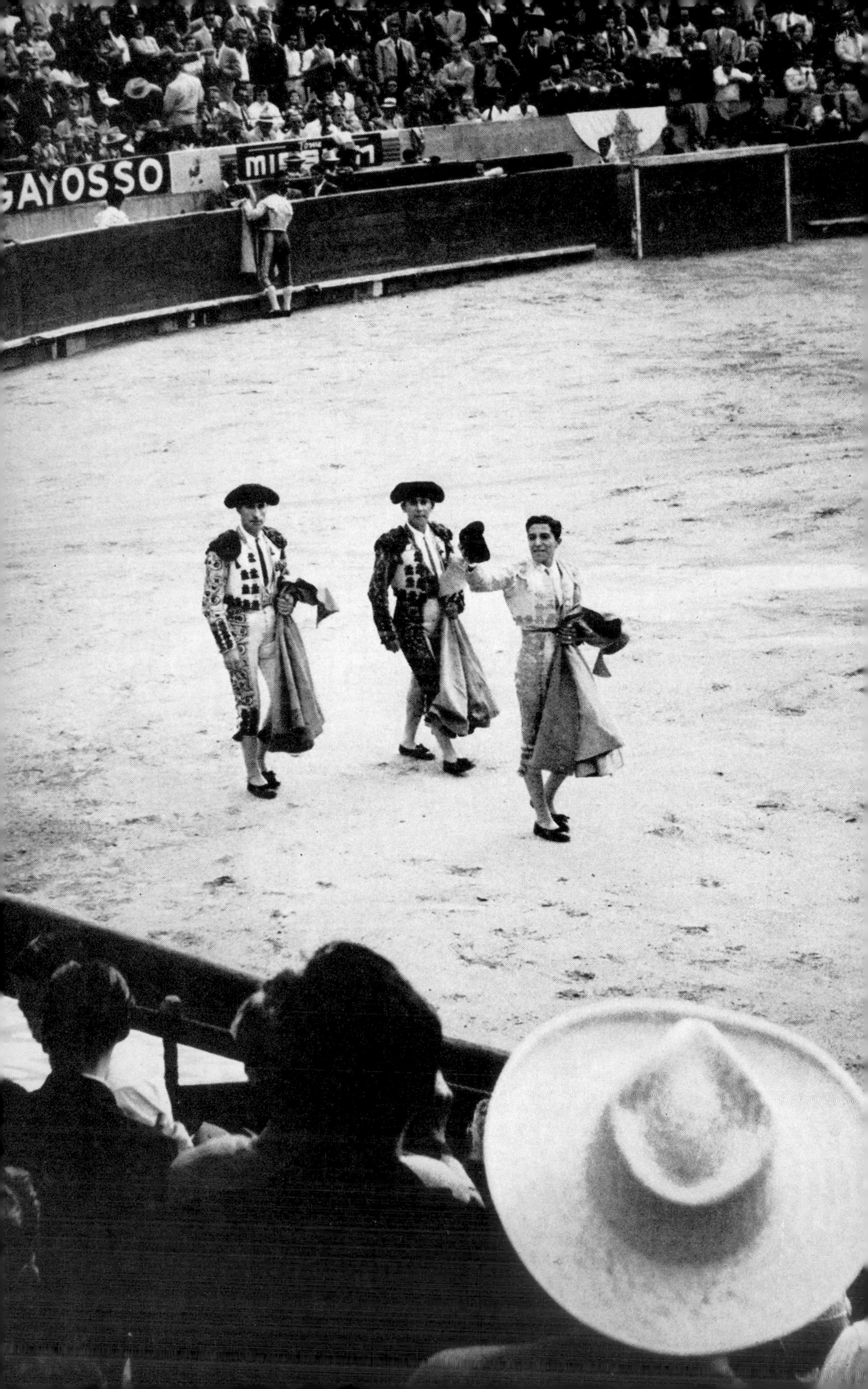
GAYOSSO

8

the

SQUARE

format

b y way of illustrating a misconception about the square format of the negative produced by the Hasselblad, I would like to recall a personal experience. It took place some twenty years ago when, as a complete fledgling in photography, I discovered a used Rolleiflex in a camera store. The camera intrigued me, and I asked the friendly clerk for his opinion of it. He explained that the camera, then about ten years old, was a "gimmick" that would never really catch on.

Why? Because of the square picture. The standard picture size for a 120 roll film camera, he explained, was 2¼ by 3¼; that in order to get twelve 2¼ by 2¼ pictures on a roll of 120 film a full inch of each negative was sacrificed.

He concluded by adding that standard *prints* were rectangular, and that, therefore, even more of each negative would have to be sacrificed in the final cropping.

What he said seemed logical, and his low opinion of this format must have reflected itself in the price of the camera, which was extremely low. It was this low price that finally motivated me to give in to my

James M. Zanutto
Hasselblad 500C, 1/250, f/11, Verichrome Pan film.

original impulse and buy the camera. I was never sorry, and found out, shortly afterward, why he was wrong.

advantage of the square format

In the first place, the image that the lens sends back to the film plane is not rectangular at all. It follows the shape of the lens, and happens to be a circle. It's true that a circular negative would be impractical to print or enlarge, if only because cropping would be a near impossibility. Therefore, the most reasonable action would be to devise a rectangular shape that would use as much as possible of the circle. The rectangular shape that does so happens to be the perfect square.

The fact of the matter is that the 2¼ by 3¼ camera sacrifices more of the circle than does the square-image one. The oblong format actually is a portion of what should be a 3¼ by 3¼ negative, the ideal format to be taken from the circle from which the 2¼ by 3¼ was taken. Since, however, the width of 120 film limits the width of the picture to 2¼ in., the circle projected on it should have a diameter no larger than what would be the diagonal of the square derived from it, with a possible slight margin.

Another fallacy commonly found in photography is represented by the standard sizes of enlarging paper. These are variations of two sets of proportions: one is the 16 by 20, the other is the 11 by 14. The basic 16 by 20 size, when cut into fourths, gives birth to the 8 by 10, which, when cut into fourths, produces the 4 by 5. The 11 by 14 is cut into fourths to bring about the 5 by 7, which is cut into fourths to make the 2½ by 3½. The result is a series of so-called *standard* printing-paper sizes: 2½ by 3½, 4 by 5, 5 by 7, 8 by 10, 11 by 14, and 16 by 20. In following this progression, one finds that no negative can be proportionately enlarged to include each of these sizes, without sacrifice to the original cropping. In other words, if a 5 by 7 is not quite big enough for the print you have in mind, and the 11 by 14 is too big, you can't just settle for the size in between, the 8 by 10, because the 8 by 10's proportions are different than those of the other two.

What's more, very few full negatives fit either of these two proportions. Therefore, in order to produce what is considered a standard print, the photographer must sacrifice some of his carefully composed negative. It would seem the more practical situation might be for all printing paper to be square, allowing the photographer to select any size or shape to suit his photograph. This would, of course, lead to a certain amount of waste of paper, but it would seem that the final print is really the thing, and the photographer could better afford to waste the trimmings of his paper than portions of his original negative, no matter how slight. In any case, the trimming could be used for test strips, or for small prints.

70

Designs by George Holton. Photo at top was made with normal 80mm lens; bottom shot was made with 60mm Distagon. He used tripods in both cases for careful composition.

What we're getting at is this. The Hasselblad photographer should not be intimidated by any standards of printing-paper manufacturers when he is composing his photograph on the ground glass. He might, if the subject demands, make use of his full square format, having in mind to produce a square print from the negative. This is achieved, of course, by using the shortest dimension of the printing paper, making an 8 by 8, or 11 by 11, or even a 16 by 16 print.

But even this should not be a restriction. The fact that the negative is a square means only that the photographer should feel completely free to take advantage of this square — of the full negative area — in composing his picture and in the final print. On the other hand, there is no reason for the photographer's not using any interesting shape he might feel the subject warrants, deriving it from the square originally made available to him. After all, composition in photography should not divorce itself from the traditions of composition that were developed during the long history of art.

(*This writer holds the opinion that photography is not, of itself, necessarily an art form, but that it may be used as an art form if considered and exploited as such.*)

No successful artist, even the most classical, distorted, or otherwise, manipulated his subject *to fit a standard size canvas*. Rather, the canvas was cut and stretched to a size and shape that lent itself most conveniently to the subject and the basic composition of the artist's interpretation of it. And yet many photographers find themselves adding to, or subtracting from, a photographic composition in order to accommodate the standard space of the negative or the final print.

composition

Even though the image is reversed, the ground-glass viewing system presents the most efficient system for careful composition. In the ground glass, the photographer can see his subject as a series of geometric shapes. In color photography, he can see the areas of color as they will appear on the final photograph; in black-and-white photography, he can, with practice, come to see the various tones and shades of black and gray and white as they will appear on the print. Manipulation of the subject is, of course, limited, when photography is compared to painting. The painter could change whole shapes, alter colors and, if necessary, move mountains, to accommodate his ideas of composition. The photographer has no such freedom, but he does have more freedom than one is prone to realize at first thought. It's true, he can move people and small, portable objects to suit himself, but the even greater freedom lies in his freedom to change the position or angle of the camera; so that two dark objects, superimposed

Murray Zinn
Hasselblad 500C, 1/250, f/2.8, Verichrome Pan film.

on each other, for instance, can be separated by moving the camera to the right or left. Foreground objects can be given height by lowering the camera; or can be reduced in comparative size by raising the camera. Background objects can be removed from the picture entirely by shifting the camera angle so that the foreground covers them. Unwanted foreground can, of course, be shot over, under or around.

Depth of field, too, is an important factor in the composition of a photograph. By throwing objects out of focus, the photographer can soften (even eliminate) their basic shapes, changing, thereby, their effect on the over-all photograph. This is particularly advantageous when the backgrounds are busy and complicated, such as foliage, and the main subjects are simple. The out-of-focus background is eliminated as a competi-

73

tive force in composition, and is used favorably to set off the sharp outlines of the subject.

It's advantageous to keep in mind that there are at least three shapes to consider in every photograph.

(1) The shape of the paper.

(2) The shape of the subject.

(3) The shape of that area of the paper that is not occupied by the subject.

The first two of these usually enter the mind of the photographer, to some extent. However, the third is seldom considered a shape, and little attention is paid to it in the taking of the photograph. And yet, this area can, and often does, make or break a picture.

In examining the over-all scene on the ground glass of his Hasselblad, the photographer would do well to consider the above-listed three factors. Composing is facilitated by the cross marked on the glass. The purpose of this cross is to present straight vertical and horizontal lines for comparison with the lines of the subject, in order to avoid distortion. But it serves the further purpose of dividing the screen into four equal sections, with a clear center spot. By imagining the final shape of the print and playing it against this cross, the photographer will find the lines are a direct aid to composition.

The subject within a photograph will, the majority of times, form one of three general shapes: a rectangle, a triangle, or a curve. The importance of these shapes within the picture can be increased or reduced by the dimensions of the final sheet of paper. A tall, narrow shape will be accentuated on a long, narrow print. By the same token, the effect (actually, strength) of the shape can be completely lost on a wide sheet of paper. The shape of the paper on which a curved subject is to be printed should depend on the direction of the curve. A horizontal curve on a vertical sheet of paper is minimized; the same goes for a vertical curve on a horizontal sheet of paper. Strength is added to the curve by printing it on a sheet of paper that coincides with its direction. More strength is given it if one end is allowed to run off the side of the paper, with the other end extending beyond the middle of the sheet. The triangle should be given the same treatment as the rectangle.

Obviously, if two shapes are to be played against each other, the larger will be the dominant. However, this too can be manipulated by the use of light or dark areas. A dark area against a light one, regardless of the difference in size, will stand out as the primary area of the composition.

One of the most successful gimmicks in being "creative" with photographic composition is the foreground frame. This is the technique used to accentuate a subject whose distance from the camera would cause it to lose strength in the over-all composition because of the size and shape of the area around it. To overcome this, an object is placed in the foreground for the express purpose of creating a third level in the picture, and reducing the nonsubject space. This third level serves to direct the viewer's eye immediately into the picture, right at the subject. Classic examples of this are the framing of a landscape with the trunk and a few branches of a tree, or framing an indoor portrait by shooting it between a couple of pillars, and through some other framing shape, such as a doorway.

The best composition is worked out carefully. In order to do this with precision, it is practical to fix your camera to a tripod, so that it will stay in exactly the place you want it to during the exposure.

The most popular composition among beginning serious photographers is simple symmetry. It's all right to play around with symmetry while finding out what you can do with your camera, but start thinking of more interesting shapes. Remember that you can print the final picture on any size sheet of paper that suits you. You are, after all, the boss. Or you become the boss as soon as you realize that the restrictions placed on your photography are artificial ones, dreamed up for the convenience of non-photographers.

contact prints and cropping

But with all the compositional advantages of the ground-glass viewing screen and the emancipation from formal paper-size restrictions, the Hasselblad photographer still has the advantage of being able to second-guess in the darkroom, or to use his enlarger to make up for physical limitations (like not being able to get close enough) of the shooting session. In fact, it's not very likely that there is a photographer in the world today who, when he enlarges his negative, prints every square centimeter of every shot he's made.

The accepted aid to cropping, today, is the contact sheet. That is, the roll of negatives is cut into three strips of four negatives each, and the entire dozen shots are printed at one time on a sheet of 8 by 10 contact paper. There are several commercial devices on the market to assist in this. However, a very acceptable method is to simply lay the negatives on a sheet of contact paper and cover the whole thing with a plate of heavy glass — heavy enough to keep the negatives flat and in perfect contact with the paper. Then expose, by room, flood, or enlarger light, and soup the entire sheet at once.

Two types of contact sheets can be made in this fashion — compensated and uncompensated. The uncompensated sheet is a straight print of the entire roll of film, with no regard being paid to the over or underexposed negatives on the roll. In other words, letting the underexposed shots go dark, the overexposed shots stay washed out, and allowing only the properly exposed negatives to make decent prints. The advantage of

Here's a section of a contact sheet from one of Jules Alexander's shooting sessions. See the last page of this book for the picture the photographer selected and how he cropped it.

this is (1) it's fast and simple, and (2) it lets you know the exact results of the exposure settings you used during the shooting. This is of particular advantage when a camera is being tested, or when you are otherwise experimenting — with film, lighting, etc.

Making a compensated contact sheet is best done by the light of the enlarger, which should be stopped down to the point where at least half a minute is required to make a decent contact print. With this extra time, you can dodge the areas of underexposure and you can burn in the areas of overexposure. The advantages here lie in (1) the fact that you will know which of your negatives are salvable by manipulation of the exposure in the enlarger, (2) that you will have a better look at the picture, and know whether or not it's worth printing, and (3) if you have to show a contact sheet to a client or customer, it's best to show him one on which all the pictures are as professional looking as possible.

76

George Holton

Most commercial custom-processing labs make contact sheets, as do many of the commercial labs catering to the amateur. These are worth having, even if you have your work done out. Besides serving as a cropping guide (which we're going to get to in a minute), they make a very handy record of what's on each roll of negatives in your file. In order to get the most out of them for record purposes, try numbering each frame with India ink and a fine pen. These black numbers, written in the clear borders of the negatives, print white on black on the contact sheets, and serve as a convenient guide. The custom labs, if you ask them, also will number your negatives (although, be warned that they charge for everything they do, and like as not they'll charge a token amount for this service, too.)

At any rate, once the contact sheets are made, study them for your compositional possibilities before projecting the negatives onto your enlarging paper. A good way to do this is to make two small L-shaped guides of cardboard. Each leg should be 2¼-in. long on its inside dimension in order to cover every possibility. Place these guides on the contact print of an individual picture in such a manner as to form a rectangle inside them. Then, if the full negative does not suit your taste, start sliding the guides together, allowing the legs to overlap each other. The inside frames formed in this manner will show you exactly how the individual shots are going to look when cropped. When you've decided on the cropping that's to be done, mark the contact with a red grease pencil. Red because it can be seen most easily under the safelight in your darkroom, and grease pencil because it can be wiped off a glossy print afterward, in case you change your mind, or in case you want to file an unmarked print.

This is an extra step in the darkroom process, but it will save you a lot of time in the long run. It will save you a bit of enlarging paper, too, since you'll do your experimenting on the contact sheet, and not in the enlarger.

Another thing that will save you a bit of enlarging paper is a magnifying glass. Often, there is movement or unsharpness from other causes on a negative, but it is so slight as to be unnoticeable on the contact. However, this slight bit of unsharpness can, when enlarged a few times, become a substantial blur on the finished print. You can avoid this by examining the contacts with a magnifying glass, which will give you a better idea of which negatives won't print adequately. There is available, in most camera stores, a magnifier with a built-in light. This is, actually, a magnifying glass which has been attached to a flashlight. It is a simple enough device, but one which comes in extremely handy. The light is projected directly onto the print, under the glass, and the shadow which might otherwise be caused by holding a magnifying glass over a print is thereby eliminated.

One service offered by the custom labs which is almost impossible to

Molly Malone Cook
Hasselblad 500C, 1/15, f/2.8, hand-held, Tri-X film.

duplicate at home, unless you happen to have an 8 by 10 enlarger, is the enlarged contact sheet. To make this, the entire roll of negatives is placed in an 8 by 10 glass negative carrier and projected onto an 11 by 14 or 16 by 20 sheet of paper. This service costs two or three dollars extra, but often it's well worth it. For one thing, there's no question of which negatives are sharp and which aren't; you can see your pictures already partially enlarged and get a much better idea of what they're going to look like; your customer gets to see prints of a size that don't smack as strongly of "amateurism" as do straight contacts, and you can cut the sheet up, after you've finished with it, to make a set of fairly good size prints. What's more, if you have a job for which you're required to show individual "proofs," these partially enlarged prints can well serve as proof prints, after being cut apart and trimmed neatly.

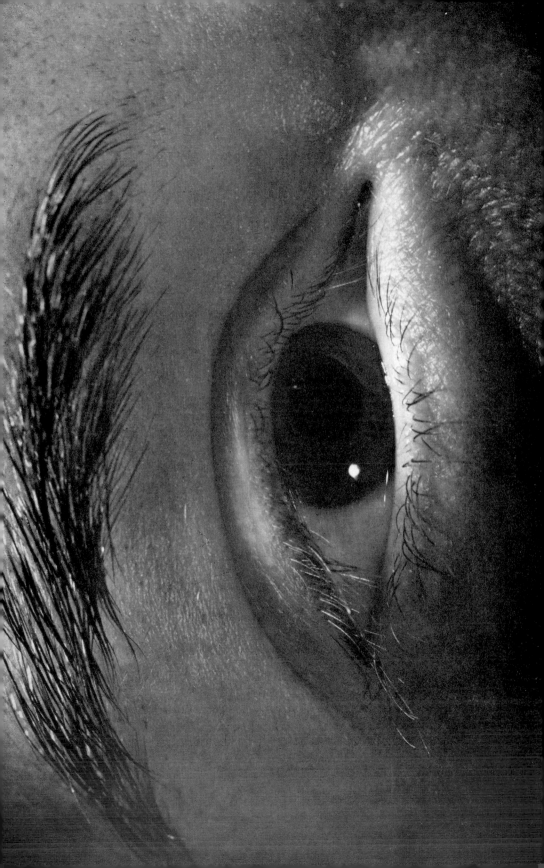

9

the

HASSELBLAD

in action

ou will find two things that make the Hasselblad the ideal small camera for portraits — (1) the square format and (2) the interchangeability of the lenses.

general portrait techniques

Cropping and composition of portraits has become a very individual thing in photography — individual to the photographer and individual to the subject. Not too long ago, a portrait was considered to be a flattering representation of the subject — the more flattering, the better. Today, flattery is secondary; the representation is the thing. A portrait must tell a story. It must emphasize certain qualities of the subject and subdue others, according to their proper values. In the quest for realism, photographers have been moving in. Whole areas of some subjects are eliminated entirely for their portraits. Hands, arms, necks, hair, and even eyes are in the picture only for what they can do. For this reason, the portrait photographer looks to the ground glass, and then uses it in terms of the format of the ultimate print. With the square viewing area, he has a choice of

Ted Russell
Hasselblad 500C, with 250mm Sonnar.

Ted Russell
Hasselblad 500C, 135mm Sonnar, studio strobes.

every possible horizontal or vertical format. And when he views through the ground glass and sees his subject through the taking lens, in exact relation to the ground glass as it will be to the printing paper, he can check on everything, position, lighting, distortion, and depth of field.

The interchangeability of the Hasselblad's lenses allows the portrait photographer to fill his negative without worrying about the distortion from being too close to, or the discomfort of being too far away from, his subject.

Probably the ideal portrait lens for *head shots* is the 135mm on the F-cameras, or the 150mm on the 500C. This lens allows him to concentrate on the composition without having to photograph things he will have to crop out of the picture in the ultimate print.

But full-length portraits are just as conveniently accomplished with this system, and without having to change camera position, or back up against the farthest wall in the studio (often, still not far enough away). The photographer merely slips on the 80mm or 60mm lens, and gets in his full length, or any props or background material he deems vital to the shot.

Of course, all these things can be done with a studio view or portrait camera. But with the small camera there is no delay (closing the shutter, stopping down manually, inserting the film holder, and pulling the slide) between the viewing/focusing and the taking. This means that the photographer is secure in the knowledge that the subject hasn't moved or otherwise changed position before the shutter is released. It means, also, that he can stimulate spontaneous expressions and positions, because he can view and focus right up to the taking of the picture, and if, after shooting, he finds the subject has finally relaxed into the pose he really wanted, the small camera photographer can, by advancing his film and rechecking his viewfinder, shoot again immediately afterward.

The Hasselblad is not as unobtrusive as a 35mm camera, but because the photographer doesn't have to hold it up to his eye, it can become less of a distraction. The subject will get used to its presence much more rapidly than he would any other studio camera.

And for really candid portraits, the Hasselblad can be used hand-held.

children's portraits

In children's portraiture, too, the trend is toward naturalism. This means, most of the time, available light. Although the Hasselblad's normal lens, $f/2.8$, is considered slow in comparison to the fast lenses of the 35mm cameras, it is fast enough to be used under *low* lighting conditions. In homes or studios, it can, if used in conjunction with today's fast films (*see the section on available light photography*), record portraits with little or no accessory light.

Head shots, as such, are not the most desirable portraits of children, because their bodies and their actions are so important to the picture. For this reason, it is not necessary to use the medium or long telephoto lenses. This is just as well, because it is best, with shutter speeds slower than 1/125 sec, to keep the camera on a tripod. The long lenses are fairly heavy, and only a tripod or a fast shutter speed will overcome the tendency toward camera shake that comes from hand-holding a long lens.

You must keep in mind, when photographing youngsters, that children must be wheedled, bluffed, seduced (as it were) into naturalness. But once they reach that state, the photographic possibilities come a mile-a-minute. The child-portrait photographer must be quick on the trigger, because as fast as a new expression or position is born, it vanishes, fades, or is replaced by another.

Another thing to keep in mind is this: Although the Hasselblad has

Les Barry
Hasselblad 500C, 60mm Distagon, 1/30, wide open, Super Hypan film.

been on the market long enough to be a famiilar sight to the camera-store browser or reader of the photography magazine ads, it *is* an unusual-looking camera — this in spite of the fact that it has won awards for the excellence of its design. Being unusual in appearance, it is bound to excite the curiosity of children. You might as well let them get used to it from up close before getting started. Else they'll delay the shooting session while they examine it from a distance.

Children are at their best, as photographic subjects, when they are completely relaxed, and children relax best in familiar surroundings or with familiar objects. Because of its portability, you can take your Hasselblad to the home of the subject, and a wide range of accessories can be tucked into your gadget bag and carried with you. If, however, you intend to shoot a child's portrait away from home, at a studio or on location, be sure to advise the parents to take along or to provide the youngster with some familiar toys. These toys, often enough, will not be things you want to have in the final photographs. You can keep them within close proximity of the youngster, but out of camera range, by keeping close tabs in the ground glass. In fact, by making the most careful use of the full viewing possibilities provided by the Hasselblad's ground-glass viewing system you can have a parent, relative, or some other person right up close to your

Jules Alexander used portable strobes to shoot this industrial illustration with his 500C and normal lens.

subject, putting him at ease, behaving perhaps in the most embarrassing manner. But you won't get the other person in the picture. You simply move in, watching your field of view, until only what you want to photograph is in the picture. Of course, you can always crop the extra person out of the print, but why waste negative space when you can avoid it.

industrial photography

The Hasselblad's two extremes in lens focal length make it a very popular camera among industrial photographers who are interested in a hand-held camera of its size. The Superwides, of course, solve countless problems for the industrial photographer. Because of its wide image angle, the Superwide can be used in crowded areas and still get everything required into the picture. In many factories, there is a definite problem caused by the small amount of area between machines. This area may not be necessarily small from the standpoint of its own particular function, but the photographer, called upon to photograph some of the gigantic machines now used in industry, would find himself at a disadvantage in not being able to get far enough away from the subject to get it all in the picture. With the Hasselblad Superwides, this is solved with an eye-level camera.

Also, the other Hasselblads, the F-cameras, do enjoy the 60mm Distagon among their accessory lenses. Although not as wide as the Superwides' 38mm Biogon, the Distagon does give enough increase in angle to solve many problems of this nature.

With either wide-angle lens, the necessity for tilts and swings on the camera is eliminated, because these cameras can be directed head-on (and perfectly straight up and down) at the subject. With a level camera, there is no convergence of lines, as occurs when a normal-lensed camera is tilted upward to include the top of a tall object. Although more than is desired might get into the picture, the excess can be cropped out, leaving an undistorted view of the subject.

In industrial photography, there is a frequent dilemma arising from the inability of the photographer to get close enough to the subject. Perhaps he's photographing a vat of hot, molten lead, or an object that's surrounded by water or mud, or just something on the side of a hill. By slipping one of the telephoto lenses on his Hasselblad, the industrial photographer overcomes the distance or barrier between the subject and his camera, and brings the subject in to negative-filling size.

The question of extreme depth of field, usually necessary in industrial photography, can be answered with the Hasselblad, too. With the Superwides, the depth of field is so great at most stops that there is no problem. With the F-cameras and the 500C, the photographer can stop down his lens and actually see the depth of field his film is going to record. Or, with the 500C, he can make use of the movable depth-of-field indicators to make sure everything is sharp, all the way back.

Taking a camera into an industrial situation can very well have a disruptive effect on the work going on, thereby costing the customer a good deal of money — the value of the lost production time. Many potential customers stay away from industrial photography for this reason. But this factor makes the Hasselblad even more popular among industrial photographers. It's small enough to be relatively unobtrusive, and the f/2.8 lens is fast enough to be used for available light photos. But even if supplementary lighting is required, the fully synced flash system of the 500C means that a photographer and an assistant, with a couple of strobes, can work out an industrial photographic problem with the smallest amount of upset to the workers around them.

Dean Vincent
Hasselblad 500C and studio strobes.

glamour and cheesecake

In addition to a pretty girl, the photographer who deals in glamour pictures today needs a hand-held camera that can be used with a long lens. Why hand-held? Because today's glamour pictures are loose and flowing; they depict action, and a hand-held camera can follow that action, thus doing away with the stilted poses of a generation ago.

Why a long lens? Today's glamour pictures close in on the models. The glamour photographer wants close-ups, but he doesn't want distortion. And, cheesecake is separated from its backgrounds; this separation is caused by limiting the depth of field, by placing the sharply outlined model against a soft background. The short (by comparison) depth of field of long lenses becomes, here, an advantage.

One other factor makes the Hasselblad the glamour photographer's delight — the interchangeable film magazine. Much of the success in glamour photography is owed to chance. The right pose, the right expression, with the light falling in the most flattering fashion, and the camera at just the proper angle — these are all elements of luck that go into making the acceptable (commercial) glamour shot. For that reason, the majority of cheesecake photographers shoot dozens of exposures at an individual sitting, with maybe just one or two photographs as the anticipated result. The Hasselblad's interchangeable film magazines give the photographer the opportunity to shoot with complete abandon. Having exposed one roll of film, he slips off one loaded magazine and snaps on another, and continues shooting for that perfect shot.

Because much of today's glamour photography takes place on location, away from the studio, and these shooting sites often are away from the beaten paths of civilization, accessible only on foot, the photographer appreciates not having to be encumbered by great loads of equipment. In fact, a camera and a loaded gadget bag would seem to be as much as any man would want to lug on one of these assignments. If the camera is a Hasselblad, the gadget bag might contain a dozen loaded magazines, and half the effort toward a successful session is eliminated. A variety of lenses, too, can be carried in the gadget bag without its having to be larger than can be carried comfortably.

With color, one other thing is needed — a source of light control. Usually, this is a reflector of some sort. There are several forms of portable reflectors available. These might be simply a stack of white cards, placed or leaned strategically around the model. A light weight folding tripod comes in handy, here, as something to lean the cards against. A tripod, also, can support the end of a roll of aluminum foil, holding it up and directing its reflection into the areas where additional illumination is needed for proper color balance.

Often, a completely candid feeling is found in a successful glamour shot. This is no accident. By making use of the portability of his camera, the photographer actually shoots a series of candid poses — usually while the model thinks she is between poses, or simply as she prepares for the session to come.

Although depth-of-field control is of paramount importance in out-

88

door cheesecake, it is just as important in the studio. Often studio assignments include props which must be in or out of focus, according to the dictates of the photographer's intention or the desire of the ultimate purchaser of the finished picture.

In the studio, too, the photographer usually likes to vary his lighting setups. He may switch from regular flash to electronic flash with the Hasselblad by the simple changing of one plug for another. And if he wants to give floods or spots a turn, he can see the exact effect of his lighting arrangements on the ground-glass viewing screen.

close-ups and macrophotography

Because of the comparative simplicity of its lens barrel system, more close-up attachments are currently available for the F-camera. However, similar attachments are being worked out for the 500C, and this chapter should, eventually, apply to both.

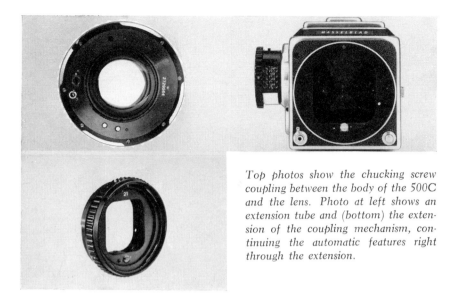

Top photos show the chucking screw coupling between the body of the 500C and the lens. Photo at left shows an extension tube and (bottom) the extension of the coupling mechanism, continuing the automatic features right through the extension.

The F-camera's lens barrel is, of course, simply a lens system and a diaphragm. The focal-plane shutter is in the rear of the camera body and, therefore, is not concerned in the application of attachments to the front or rear of the lens barrel. With the 500C, on the other hand, a different situation exists because of the Compur shutter (1) being in the lens barrel, and (2) being coupled to a release button that is in the camera body. Any attachment can be placed on the front of this lens barrel without operational problems, but in placing an attachment on the rear of the lens barrel, between the lens and the camera body, some provisions must be made to extend the coupling from the shutter (and automatic diaphragm mechanism) to the shutter-release button located on the camera body.

Normally, when a lens is attached to the 500C body, the shutter and diaphragm are immediately related to the body-release and film-transport mechanism by means of a slotted chucking-shaft arrangement. This chucking shaft must transfer two operations from the body to the lens barrel, opening the shutter and diaphragm when the film is advanced, stopping down the diaphragm and operating the shutter when the body release is pressed. The problem represented here is solved with the 500C in a simple but efficient fashion. An actual fine steel rod runs through each extension tube for the 500C. This rod is fitted, at each end, with the regular lens-fitting pieces. These pieces couple to the lens barrel and the shaft-end on the camera body. The result is that the action is transferred from the camera body to the lens barrel by the simple movement of the rod between them. At this writing, there exists a bellows attachment for the F-cameras, and a bellows attachment for the 500C is promised. The bellows

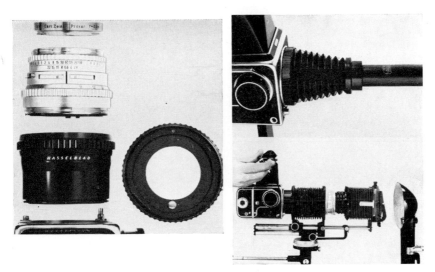

Full line of Hasselblad extension tubes, bellows and microscope adapter add to camera's versatility.

for the 500C is expected to include a coupling arrangement similar to that of the extension tubes, except for a more flexible connecting rod.

Simple close-ups for both types of Hasselblad reflex cameras can be made with the attachment of close-up or Proxar lenses. The series includes two lenses, a 1-meter lens and a 0.5-meter lens. These, of course, indicate the minimum distance between camera and subject possible. These minimum distances apply to the normal lens, but the Proxars also may be used with the telephoto lenses, with similar advantage.

Extension tubes extend the lens focal length to permit closing in on a subject. Also available are microscope adapters, which permit these cameras to be used for taking pictures directly through the microscope lens.

The bellows, a fine-focusing, double-track, long-extending unit of the Novoflex type, also provides a bellows-type sunshade. The sunshade serves a double purpose by serving as a holder for color slides which are to be copied. The two bellows can be extended to provide a one-to-one relationship between the material to be copied and the film plane of the camera.

To calculate the increase in exposure that is necessitated by the extension of the bellows, scales are provided for each focal length of lens. These scales, engraved on the rear track, are in the form of a notching code. Each notch denotes a doubling of exposure time.

Fast film (Ansco Super Hypan), rated at 800 ASA, made possible this room-light (single 60-watt lamp), available light home portrait by Les Barry. Hasselblad 500C, 1/30, f/2.8.

10

available
LIGHT--FILM
speed

W hat, ask the purists, is available light photography? And how does it differ from existing light photography, or, for that matter, bad light photography? And when the lighting, regardless of how *available*, is moved, shaded, or otherwise manipulated, does this continue to be available light photography? The popular answers to these questions go from one philosophic extreme to the other. Personally, I go for the explanation given by H. M. Kinzer, in his book, *Kinzer's Available Light Photography,** where he describes the function of available light photography as an effort to "preserve the quality of the natural situation, and to avoid intruding on it." If by slightly changing an existing lighting setup, or the subject's relationship to it, the photographer can improve a photograph, he has not necessarily removed the shot from the category of available light. However, to define available light further for the purpose of discussion in this chapter, let's stipulate what it is *not*. It is not so-called "natural" light photography, which would refer to the relatively normal daylight of outdoor photography during the normal daylight hours. Nor is it studio lighting, studio lighting being the use of floods, spots, or flash for the principal source of light. What's left, then, *is* available light.

* New York: Universal Photo Books, 1958.

Shallow depth of field added to the charm of the top photo by Ted Russell. For bottom photo Les Barry stopped down to f/5.6, mounted camera on a tripod and used 1/15 of a second exposure.

We combine available light photography and the use of film in one chapter in this book, because it is the feeling of this author that the manufacturers of film have been to a large extent responsible for the progress of available light photography, particularly in the 2¼ camera. In the modern history of available light photography, it is generally agreed that the field was founded by Dr. Erich Salomon who, in about 1928, began using an Ermanox camera to photograph famous people in situations in which flash powder would have been disruptive. The Ermanox had an $f/2$ lens (considered miraculous), but film speed in those days was slow; hence, Dr. Salomon usually was restricted to very slow shutter speeds. At about the time the Ermanox was introduced, Oskar Barnack placed on the market his invention, the Leica. The first Leicas, though, were no faster than $f/3.5$. It wasn't until the early thirties that the Leica factory broke the $f/3.5$ barrier with an $f/1.9$ lens, and the camera went on to become the grandfather of today's available light photography.

For many years the bulk of available light work was done with a miniature camera of Leica (35mm) size, because it was only with these cameras that lenses of $f/2$ and faster were practical and economical.

This situation still exists, but in the last twenty years film speed has become gradually faster. In the last five years a major revolution has taken place, giving film such high ratings that the 2¼'s usual $f/3.5$ lens, or the most recent $f/2.8$ lens, as found on the Hasselblad, has become suitable for available light work. And as fast as films are, photographers now, as a general practice, increase their speeds by underexposing and overdeveloping. In fact, the manufacturers, themselves, now admit to the latitude included in the ratings they give their films. Things have progressed to the extent that photographers no longer consider the manufacturers' ratings to be the ideal or recommended ones for their favorite films. Many professionals and advanced amateurs find themselves determining their own film-speed ratings, based on their individual exposure and development procedure. Influential here, too, is the choice of prepared developers.

film guide

Of the high-speed films, those most suitable for the most extreme available light conditions (by extreme, we mean the least amount of usable light), there is a close competition between Eastman Kodak's Royal-X Pan and the German Agfa Isopan Record. Royal-X is rated, by the manufacturer, at 650 ASA, but even Kodak warns that using this film at its rated speed is liable to result in overexposure. The recommended speed is somewhere between 1250 and 1600 ASA, for a normal type overdevelopment, but Royal-X has been used at speeds upward of 2000 ASA with reasonable results.

Ted Russell used fast films, Super Hypan for photo on this page, Tri-X for photo on opposite page, to make these two Times Square shots with a Hasselblad 500C.

Isopan Record is manufacturer-rated at 640 ASA, but no one seems inclined to use it at a speed anywhere near that *low*.

In testing Isopan Record when it was first introduced, Bob Schwalberg, technical editor of *Popular Photography* magazine, exposed this film at indexes ranging from 1600 to 8000 ASA. He found that although he got pictures at every rating, the highest, 6000 to 8000, were considered "last resort," because the overdevelopment produced more grain than was considered acceptable, and blocked up in the bright highlight areas. He recommended that maximum quality was obtained when this film was exposed for an index of 1600 to 2400 ASA, and that printable negatives of low-contrast subjects were obtained when the film was rated between 3200 and 4000 ASA.

But both Isopan Record and Royal-X are beyond what is necessary for available light photography. Film speeds of 400 to 1000 ASA, cer-

Cameras were hand-held in both shots, although light from theater marquee allowed him to stop down and get slight depth-of-field bonus.

tainly adequate, can be obtained from the slower group of fast films, with much better quality and much less grain. Ansco Super Hypan, for instance, although rated by the manufacturer at 200 ASA, is considered ideal, as to grain and quality, when rated between 650 and 100 ASA. Kodak Tri-X Pan, once considered amazing because the company put it on the market with a 200 ASA label, is usually used at twice that speed, and then some. The same goes for Gevaert Gevapan 36.

Several European manufacturers have introduced a new twist in panchromatic films, making them usable at faster tungsten speeds than daylight speeds. Some of these are Agfa Isopan Ultra, 250 daylight, 400 tungsten; Guilleminot Guilpan, 160 daylight, 200 tungsten; and Perutz Peromnia 25, 250 daylight, 320 tungsten.

However, in all of the cases listed above, there is more film speed than is necessary for most available light photography. And, as is to be expected, the extra speed results in a compensatory loss of quality and increase in grain. In most cases, adequate speed for available light work can be found in the so-called medium-speed films, which show a minimum of grain, with extremely good quality, even when pushed.

Adox R21, manufacturer rated at 80 ASA, is one of the most outstanding of these. Exposed at twice that speed, it gives quality comparable to the slower of the films of other manufacturers. However, little difference, in normal-size blow-ups, is apparent between it and Kodak Verichrome Pan, which has the identical rating, and which can be doubled with just as much ease.

Since the introduction of Super Anscochrome film, available light color photography has become a practical affair. This film is produced in both a daylight and tungsten type, and each is indexed at 100. However, commercial custom processing labs have proven themselves capable of over-developing this film, with only slight increase in grain, making ratings of 200 quite practical.

Since film speed has eliminated any question of the Hasselblad's possibilities as an available light camera, only one obstacle remains, and this can be overcome by the user who is willing to meet the camera half-way. That is the problem of focusing in bad light. This requires some ingenuity. In practically any available light situation there must exist some high-light. It is on this highlight, even if it's only a glint in a subject's eye, that the photographer must learn to focus if he's going to use his ground glass to focus with. Ground-glass focusing in bad light is facilitated by the use of the critical-focusing hood. This magnifies the image, while eliminating any extraneous glare which might interfere with the best use of the ground glass. One other avenue is open to the Hasselblad user who turns to bad light photography — the careful use of his depth-of-field scale. If he pays attention to these movable pointers, he'll find that depth of field is his greatest ally here. To explain, at close range, he should have little difficulty focusing on the ground glass. However, distant subjects appear too small on the ground-glass screen for really sharp pinpoint focusing. But, when the subject is further distant from the camera, the depth of field increases. By paying attention to this, and either estimating distance by eye, or loosely focusing before and behind the subject to determine approximate distance, and covering this distance by the movable depth-of-field pointers, he can eliminate the anticipated difficulties.

Here is a roundup of 120 film, available for the Hasselblad in this country, at the time of this writing. Ordinarily, black-and-white film falls into three speed classifications. It would seem that today's developments have created a fourth, which we include here. The film speeds given are those of the manufacturers. However, in most cases, these ratings may be at least doubled for more versatility.

98

		ASA RATINGS	
MANUFACTURER	FILM	DAYLIGHT	TUNGSTEN

Class I — Slow Film — Very Fine Grain

Manufacturer	Film	Daylight	Tungsten
Adox	R14	16	12
	R17	40	25
Agfa	Isopan FF	20	16
	Isopan F	40	32
Gevaert	Gevapan 27 Microgran	32	20
Kodak	Panatomic-X	25	20

Class II — Medium Speed Film — Moderate Grain

Manufacturer	Film	Daylight	Tungsten
Leitz	Adox R21	80	64
Agfa	Isopan SS	100	80
Ansco	All Weather Pan	65	50
Gevaert	Gevapan 30	64	40
	Gevapan 33	125	80
Ilford	FP3	64	50
Kodak	Verichrome Pan	80	64
	Plus-X Pan	80†	64†
Konica	Konipan S	50	40
	Konipan SS	100	80
Perutz	Perpantic 18	50	40
	Peromnia 21	100	100
Mimosa	Panchroma 17	100	80

Class III — Fast Film — Substantial Grain

Manufacturer	Film	Daylight	Tungsten
Agfa	Isopan Ultra	250	400
Ansco	Super Hypan	200	160
Gevaert	Gevapan 36	250	160
Ilford	Guilpan	160	200
Guilleminot	HP3	200	160
Kodak	Tri-X	200	160
Konica	Konipan SSS	200	160
Perutz	Peromnia 25	250	320
Mimosa	Panchroma 21	250	160

Class IV — High-Speed Film — Extreme Grain

Manufacturer	Film	Daylight	Tungsten
Agfa	Isopan Record	640	500
Kodak	Royal-X Pan	650	

COLOR

Manufacturer	Film	Daylight	Tungsten
Ansco	Anscochrome	32	12*
	Super Anscochrome (Daylight)	100	40*
	Super Anscochrome (Tungsten)	80*	100

---

† Manufacturer recommends one stop less exposure.
* With conversion filter.

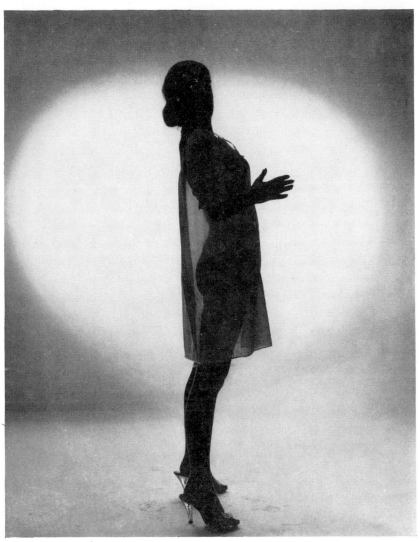

Dean Vincent
Hasselblad 500C, 1/30, f/8, two spots on background.

Kodak	Ektachrome (Daylight)	32	12*
	Ektachrome (Type F)	16	20
	Ektachrome Professional	50	
	Kodacolor	32	25*
Konica	Konicolor	10	

Decamired filters

In using color film, there is more to consider than just the film's Exposure Index. The matter of color temperature is introduced, and for the critical color photographer Hasselblad has come up with a set of light balancing filters based on the Decamired system. (Please note that, in photographic terms, the higher the temperature, the colder the color.)

The easiest way to use Decamired filters is, of course, to use a color-temperature meter. The meter is set according to the temperature of the film being used, and a reading of the light source is taken. The meter then indicates a *plus* or *minus* value, indicating that the temperature of the light entering the lens must be raised or lowered to coincide with the temperature of the film — for the most accurate color reproduction. With the Hasselblad Decamired filters, lowering the temperature is accomplished by the addition of a filter colored to a degree of brownish red, while raising the temperature is accomplished by the addition of a filter colored to a degree of blue. This may seem to be the opposite of the desired effect, and, as a matter of fact, it is. In photography the function of a filter is to add a color. Therefore, a blue filter will add blue to the light passing through the lens, thereby cooling the color; the opposite is true for a brownish-red filter.

The blue, or minus, filters are designated CB. The reddish, or plus filters, are designated CR. Each type comes in a series of three, viz: CB 1.5, CB 3, and CB 6; and CR 1.5, CR 3, and CR 6. Therefore, if the color temperature should indicate a -3, you would use the CB 3 filter; if a $+6$, you would use the CR 6 filter.

In addition to the six filters described above, there are available, also, a CB 12 and a CR 12 filter. They are not sold with the basic kits. They are usable as straight conversion filters, since the CB 12 converts daylight film for use by tungsten light, and CR 12 converts tungsten-type film for use in daylight.

It should be pointed out, too, that the Hasselblad Decamired filters are double-bayoneted. This means that the filters, in addition to being bayonet-mounted to the lens, may be bayonet-mounted to each other. The result is that more than one filter may be used at a time, and the effect is that of the combined numbers. For instance, a CB 1.5 and a CB 3 filter, combined, would have the effect of a CB 4.5. In this regard, many combinations are possible.

Two sets of numbers are engraved on the rim of each filter. One is the CB or CR number, and the second is the filter factor. Each Decamired filter, with the exception of the 1.5 filters and the CR 3, reduces the amount of light entering the lens, and the exposure must be increased accordingly. For instance, the CB 6 has a filter factor of 2, which means exposure must be doubled.

The CR 3 is the equivalent of a skylight filter.

Color temperature of film and light is measured in degrees Kelvin (K). Daylight-type film is balanced at 5,800 K; tungsten type-film is balanced at 3,200 K.

If it were just a matter of using daylight-type film outdoors and

Charles Reynolds
Hasselblad 500C, 1/30, f/2.8, Tri-X film.

tungsten-type film indoors, there would be no problem. However, the color temperature of the light sources varies to a large extent. The position of the sun in the sky, the time of day, the weather, all affect the Kelvin temperature of the light. The various types of tungsten lamps have varying Kelvin temperatures.

Here are some typical Kelvin temperatures:

Clear sky and sunshine	5,800 K
Cloudy sky	6,500 K
Overcast sky	7,500 K
Electronic flash	6,500 K
Early morning, late afternoon sunlight	5,000 K
Clear flashbulbs	3,800 K
Photofloods	3,400 K
Studio floods	3,200 K
100-watt household lamps	2,700 K

So now we know the Kelvin temperatures of both film and the light sources. How, then, do we bring them together through the Decamired system? Both film and light sources have, in addition to Kelvin temperatures, Decamired values. The Decamired value is determined by dividing the number 100,000 by the Kelvin temperature. In doing so we eliminate the fraction numbers and bring the D/M value to the nearest full number. When you know that you can select the proper Decamired filter without the use of a color-temperature meter.

For example, the color temperature of both daylight and daylight-type film is 5,800 K. We divide this number into 100,000 and get 18 (plus a slight fraction, which we drop). Suppose, then, that we are going to shoot a roll of daylight-type film during an overcast day. The temperature of daylight when the sky is overcast is 7,500 K. This, when divided into 100,000, gives us a D/M value of 13. Subtracting 13 from 18, we find the daylight must be warmed by 5, so we slip the − 1.5 and the − 3 D/M filters on the camera. (The total of the two is 4.5, rather than 5, but color film has a latitude of about 500 K, which means a tolerance of up to 2 Decamired units, plus or minus.)

Wratten filters

If you are used to using Wratten-type filters, here is a list of comparative values:

WRATTEN		D/M	
80 C		CB	7.5
80 B		CB	12
80		CB	13.5
85 C		CR	9
82 B		CB	3
82 C		CB	4.5
82		CB	1.5
85		CR	12
85 B		CR	13.5
81 B		CR	3
81 C		CR	4.5
81		CR	1.5

Why, since Wratten filters already exist, has the Decamired system been worked out? Simply this: A Wratten filter used at one color temperature will not produce the same change in degrees Kelvin when used at another temperature. Decamired filters, on the other hand, have a uniform effect, making the same amount of change in one temperature of light as it will in another. And, conveniently enough, Decamired filters can be combined for greater versatility and variety of effects.

11

when you get a

HASSELBLAD

in your hands...

*a*n interesting thing I've heard from several photographers who switched to Hasselblads is that previous to changing cameras their photographic development had reached a certain impasse, a point of non-progress, as it were. Then, when they got their hands on Hasselblads, they found that new vistas of photography had opened for them, that they were taking off in new directions, that their pictures had become fresh again, and that they were experiencing a new surge of aesthetic growth. In trying to analyze this, they, and sometimes I, have considered the possibility that the Hasselblad was a technically better camera than what they had been using, or that it was more versatile. But this did not seem to provide the full answer, since the development was, for the most part, not really technical; and it has taken place with photographers who are most restrained about taking advantage of the Hasselblad's accessories or versatility. The answer, then, seemed to lie in this simple fact — the Hasselblad is a *different* camera.

George Holton

George Holton has made a papier mâché false lens which he attaches to the winding nob of his Hasselblad 1000F, is able to take portraits like this while seeming to be photographing in another direction.

camera differences

It's different in design and function from anything that existed on the market before its introduction, and it remains substantially different from all the other cameras used by professionals and advanced amateurs. This difference is immediately apparent from the time you see your first Hasselblad in the camera store window. It becomes still more obvious the first time you get your hands on one. Its design seems to be the best existing example in photography of the theory that *form follows function.* Nothing about its design would seem to be based on anything as fundamental as camera history or tradition. Instead, it seems to have been conceived as an instrument that begins with a lens, which is followed by a light-tight box, and ends with a surface of film. And all other embellishments appear to be only functional ones.

When you first hang a Hasselblad from its strap around your neck, you are quite aware that it hangs with its lens pointing down. This strikes many people as an unfortunate thing, because the camera is felt to be not quite ready for pictures — as ready as one whose lens faces outward. Yet, the camera is so balanced that the first touch of any of its controls, preparatory to taking a picture, gives you enough leverage to swing its lens upward and out.

Courtesy Victor Hasselblad AB

Why, then, does it hang lens down? This position is another of the many safety factors on the camera. By hanging down, the lens is shielded from practically all common accidents of the collision variety; and it's protected from dirt and precipitation. What's more, by hanging lens downward, the camera protrudes only about a third as far as it would otherwise, and can be buttoned under a loose-fitting coat.

Finally, instead of slowing down the time it takes to get your camera into action, this position actually speeds it up, because with the lens down, it's much safer and more practical to carry the camera without a lens cap, and with filters and sunshade attached; or, the camera can be worn around the neck with a telephoto lens attached, with no more bulge than usual.

I might point out that I do not recommend carrying any camera without a lens cap, and that I mention, simply, that this precarious practice is safer with the Hasselblad than with most other cameras.

When you begin to use any reflex camera with a focusing and viewing screen, you find yourself more aware of the arrangement of things in photographic terms, even when you see them without the aid of the

107

George Holton

camera. This is a gradual process that comes to the Hasselblad user. Also, with the aid of the ground-glass screen, you become more aware of the function and performance of light as it relates to photography, as well as the simple business of simply seeing things. To the casual photographer, these can be world-shaking experiences, and it seems almost necessary to advise caution in making use of these two new awarenesses.

the first pictures

More than likely, your first pictures with a new camera will be made outdoors. This is considered *testing* the camera, but in actuality it is getting to know its possibilities. The quality and infinite variety of outdoor natural light provides the greatest number of possibilities for seeing just what the camera will do.

Use your first few rolls of film to test the depth of field and the various opportunities opened for you by the freedom of depth-of-field manipulation. Try simple outdoor portraits. Use your ground glass to relate your subjects to their backgrounds. Because you have the advantage of being able to view with the taking lens, you can line up your subjects and their backgrounds for the most advantageous compositional possibilities.

Your first portraits will, quite naturally, be close-ups. Be careful to avoid distortions inherent in pictures of this nature. These will disappear, of course, as you increase the distance between the camera and the subject for more complex portraits — those in which more than the subjects' faces are being recorded. As you move back, you'll find yourself treading on more and more dangerous ground, because the more of the subject that gets into the photograph the more care the photographer must exercise in relating it to the background. A head, for instance, has only one basic shape. A head and shoulders, though, becomes a more complex shape, and must be dealt with accordingly. But an entire body, with arms and legs visible and positioned for realism, becomes a series of shapes, and breaks up the rest of the photograph's format into a second series of shapes. Which of these becomes the lesser in importance is part of the photographer's burden and prerogative. A complicated subject can become completely lost against a complicated background. How do you control this? By using your freedom to change camera angle, and by taking advantage of your full range in choice of depth of field.

An interesting new trend has appeared in photography recently: and it's one which, if not overdone, can make a substantial contribution to photography as an art medium. This trend, I might point out, seems to come from the activities of single-lens reflex photographers, exercising their freedom to focus selectively. Their viewpoint was summed up quite cogently by Y. Ernest Satow, who, in an article in *Popular Photography* magazine, said, "Although most fans of the SLR system laud it because it shows the photographer the exact area *in* focus, I am more taken by the fact that I can observe the exact area that's *out* of focus." It is this out-of-focus area, previously considered a by-product of photography, that has become very important to many of the newer photographers. They photograph it. They photograph it because with the single-lens reflex they are able to *see* it, and, after all, photographing what you're able to see is really basic in photography.

Satow and others have been taking pictures in which the main subject is completely, but deliberately, out of focus. They find in these abstract-type results, an opportunity to be interpretive and creative in their photography. And this technique is being used even in portraiture, with the result that a portrait of a person can become simply a mood or other such impression given off by this person. This is precarious business, undoubtedly, but when it's successful, it's really successful.

This technique is as easy to accomplish with the F-cameras as with the 500C, since both can be stopped down manually, allowing the photographer to see his depth of field at any aperture. However, even this is of limited importance in so-called out-of-focus photography, because only the shortest depths of field are used, since cameras usually are operated wide open.

And don't sell short the depth-of-field scale on the lens barrel for this type of photography. In fact, critical depth-of-field pictures might become even easier to make when you get used to using this system. As explained previously, you focus on the closest spot you want in focus, and make a note, mental or otherwise, of its exact distance from the camera. Then you focus on the farthest spot you want in focus, and find out its exact distance from the camera. Now, without even bothering to examine the image on the ground glass, you adjust the lens barrel and/or aperture and/or shutter speed (this is simpler than it might sound) so that the two red pointers on the depth of field scale are set on those two exact points — the nearest and the farthest. If you are surprised, it will be favorably so when you find, upon examining the negative or print, that your depth of field is exactly as you wanted it to be.

As you practice with this system, or if you just check your distance on the scale every once in a while, while making a picture, you will find in time that you have become reasonably proficient in judging distances between camera and subject. This ability, plus a facility for the zone-focusing method described above, will come in very handy when you use the sportsfinder, completely free of the ground-glass system; when you take other fast-action pictures, with or without the sportsfinder; or when you take available light pictures in which it is difficult to focus accurately because there's not enough light on the subject.

110

One of the things you don't have to worry about with the Hasselblad is the position of the sun. Now that the myth, "All pictures must be taken with the sun behind the camera," has been worn out and discarded, there is a danger of reflections, fog, and ghosts appearing on the film because of the sun's rays having entered the lens, either directly or by bounce. This is not a danger to the single-lens reflex photographer, for the reason, mentioned before, that the photographer sees exactly what enters his lens. If the sun should be slipping in in such a manner as to spoil an otherwise good picture, the SLR photographer knows about it before he trips the shutter, because he sees it on the ground glass. For this reason, you can use your Hasselblad to add another note of interest to your photographs — the freedom to use back and side lighting creatively, without having to worry about the possibility of the light's spoiling the picture.

And although front lighting is considered simpler and is still more popular than any other, it too has its disadvantages, and the SLR's ground glass can help you overcome them. Specifically, front lighting has two unfavorable effects, particularly in portraiture. If it is too low, too near camera level, it will flatten out the subject by flooding it with highlight, and cause the subject to lose much of its modeling and/or perspective. Flat portrait lighting of this nature is one of the surest ways to spoil an otherwise interesting portrait. If, on the other hand, the front lighting is too high, it will create deep and cavernous shadows in and around the eyes, cheeks, under the nose, and in any other area of depression.

The ground-glass screen helps you avoid these two failings because they are as apparent on the ground glass as they would be on the finished print. Once you've seen and become aware of them, you've won 90 per cent of the battle of eliminating them.

12

what about

ACCESSORIES?

*f*ortunately, before putting any model on the market the Hasselblad people have made sure that a long list of accessories was available for it. Naturally, some of these extras and attachments fall into the category of "luxuries." Others, though, come as virtual necessities, and it is their availability that makes any Hasselblad the versatile camera that it is.

extra magazines and lenses

One of the most popular accessories, and justifiably so, is the extra roll-film magazine. These magazines, both the 12-exposure and the 16-exposure models, sell for about $80 each. Whether or not this is a lot of money is relative, and depends, naturally, on its value to the individual photographer. There are some professional photographers who have dozens of these magazines. To them, the opportunity to change film in an instant; the freedom to change emulsions, in the middle of a roll of film, to suit the individual shot; and the possibilities for immediate back-and-forth switching from black-and-white to color are worth many times the price of the extra film backs involved. Often, the one shot saved by not having to wait to rewind and reload earns the price of several magazines.

Lens interchangeability is one of the features that sets single-lens

Murray Zinn
Hasselblad 500C, 1/500, f/5.6, Verichrome Pan film.

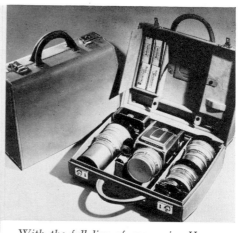

With the full line of accessories, Hasselblad offers a full line of cases in addition to the Eveready case, bottom left. The others are typical of the selection for carrying one or more cameras with extra lenses and accessories.

reflex photography apart as a successful system in its own right. Accessory lenses for the F-cameras are available at prices ranging from about $180 for the 60mm Distagon to about $300 for the 250mm Sonnar. Extra lenses for the 500C are somewhat higher, starting at about $310 and going up to about $330. Why are the 500C's lenses more expensive? Mainly, because each lens contains its own built-in synchronized Compur shutter and automatic diaphragm. Some potential Hasselblad users have complained that it did not seem economical to have to buy an extra shutter each time they bought an extra lens. Be this as it may, other photographers have been grateful, on location and at other times, for the fact that each lens contains its own shutter, because they would not be inclined, ordinarily, to carry extra shutters along as part of their kit. Previously, when a shutter needed repair an entire camera was put out of commission. On a trip or on location, the having of extra shutters in the extra lenses has meant the difference between getting pictures and not getting pictures, since a broken shutter was made up for, temporarily to be sure, by the use of a lens of another focal length and its shutter. Even in studio work, when a shutter goes out of commission the camera is tied up for at least a couple of days, and often longer. Not so with the Hasselblad 500C. The shutter requiring repair is sent off for service, and another lens stands by to take over if the occasion should arise.

All in all, the combination of extra magazines and extra lenses is tantamount to having extra cameras on hand.

other accessories

The film-advance knob, with built in exposure meter, is a $27-accessory that's priced in the neighborhood of a decent meter. There's no question about the fact that if you don't own a meter you ought to get one. If you happen to own a Hasselblad 500C anyway, you might as well get an exposure-meter knob. This is a small, but quite sensitive, meter made in Germany by the Gossen works. It is calibrated for the 500C's EVS scale, with a mirror built right under the needle to make pinpoint readings comfortable. A sliding white screen can be moved over the cell for incident-light readings, or the cell can be bared for reflected light readings. The meter's EVS reading is transferred directly to the EVS scale on the lens barrel, and facilitates the taking and setting of exposure values. Because of its interchangeability, the meter, which slips off the camera body at the sliding of a lever, can be used off the camera for critical readings in restricted areas. Often, this is more comfortable than having to stick the camera right under a subject's nose, and certainly it's more practical than having to move a tripod-mounted camera.

The fast-advance crank is another accessory that fits onto the camera in place of the winding knob. This $15-accessory is considered particularly valuable to sports photographers who want to advance the film and cock the shutter in a hurry for sequence-type shots. It's a folding crank (folds up against the camera body when not in use) that completes its winding and allied functions all in one forward motion.

Probably the accessory next most important to the Hasselblad owner is a tripod. Although Hasselblad doesn't manufacture a line of tripods, there are many good sturdy tripods on the market, and the Hasselbladder would do well to invest in one at the earliest, particularly if he is interested in using telephoto lenses. A tripod also is valuable to the Hasselblad user who wants to make the most of the compositional advantages offered by the camera's ground-glass viewing system.

Hasselblad does offer a quick-coupling attachment for the 500C. The 500C's base plate has, in addition to two tripod screw holes (one for European-size screws and one for American), a bracket for the quick coupler. This coupler screws on the tripod, as would a camera, and the camera is locked to it by a lever-operated track along its side. Attaching or removing the camera is the work of an instant.

No accessory viewing device is needed for the efficient operation of any model Hasselblad. The regular focusing hood of the F-cameras and the 500C, with its built-in magnifier, should fill any ordinary photographic need. However the accessory devices are available for (1) the perfection-ist, or (2) the unusual photographic problem.

The magnifying hood ($37.50) with its adjustable eyepiece is par-ticularly valuable for macro and micro photography, or other close-up

Newly added to the accessory list are the Hasselblad grips, shown above. The grip at left has a trigger which operates the shutter release; grip at right accommodates cable release and flash bracket. Below is the quick-action tripod head.

work in which depth of field is critical to the fraction of an inch. With this hood, the finest ground-glass focusing is possible. Also, the hood eliminates the bother of having to deal with extraneous light which might fall on the ground glass and interfere with focusing and vewing.

The Superwide actually comes without any viewing device. The reflecting viewfinder is considered an accessory, and sells for $49. Many Superwide owners prefer to use this camera solely as a studio camera, and find it more practical to use a ground-glass back for the most perfect arrangement, distortion control, and control of depth of field. The ground-glass back ($19.50) mounts to the back of the camera in place of the film magazine. Either a magnifying hood or a standard focusing hood ($28.50), the same as fits on the top of the F-cameras and the 500C, may be fitted to the ground-glass back. However, a regular focusing cloth should serve the purpose in studio work.

For close-up work, here is a list of accessories available, and their approximate prices:

FOR THE 500C ONLY

Lens Mount Adapter	$13.50
Extension Tube	36.00
Microscope Adapter	21.60
Proxar Lens, 1-meter	11.50
Proxar Lens, 0.5-meter	11.50

FOR THE 1000F ONLY

Extension Tube #20	$19.00
Extension Tube #40	21.00
Bellows Extension	115.50
Microscope Adapter	24.00

Filters for the 500C are fitted for bayonet-mounting to the front of the lens. The F-cameras and the Superwide both have screw-threaded lens fronts, and each lens comes with an outside screw ring for holding filters in place. Filters available for the normal and telephoto lenses for the 1000F are yellow, yellow-green, green, orange, red, and haze. These sell for $8.95 each. Available for the 1000F's 60mm lens, as well as for the Superwide, are yellow, green, orange, red, and haze filters. These cost $12.95 each. In addition to the filters listed above, there is a polarizing filter ($24.35) and a diffuson screen (6.33) for the F-camera's normal and telephoto lenses.

The set of filters used for the Superwide and the 1000F's 60mm lens is also used for the 500C's 60mm lens. For the 500C's 80mm, 150mm, and 250mm lenses there are yellow, yellow-green, green, orange, red, and haze filters, which cost $9.25. The diffusion screen is $11.80 and the polarizer is $29.75.

Decamired filters, which fit on the 500C's normal and telephoto lenses, come in a set of six, which sells for $72.60. This includes the CR1.5, CR3, CR6, CB1.5, CB3, and CB6. The CR12 and CB12 are sold separately for $12.10 each.

A bayonet adapter ring, to permit the 500C to take other Series VIII filters, will be available soon. Such a ring is currently available for the Superwide and the 60mm Distagon lenses, and sells for $3.20.

C
H
A
P
T
E
R

13

on

SUMMING UP

$\mathcal{M}$y intention, in preparing this book, was not to give the impression that the Hasselblad is necessarily *the* ideal camera. It is, though, an extraordinary camera, one which filled a decided gap in photography, and one which has played and is playing an important part in the development of photography as an art, a science, and a profession. Perhaps one of the surest signs of its success was the introduction of more than one new 120-size single-lens reflex some dozen years after Hasselblad pioneered its way onto the scene and established itself as a very acceptable system for taking pictures. In fact, one of the new cameras looks very much like the Hasselblad, and incorporates a good number of its basic features — interchangeable backs, etc. And yet, many substantial functional differences exist between the two makes. Some of the new 120 SLR's, like the 500C, have automatic diaphragms.

There's no likelihood that all cameras of the future will be single-lens reflexes, but there's no disguising the fact that the SLR's popularity has increased by leaps and bounds over the course of a few years, and that manufacturers of 35mm cameras have come to place more and more emphasis on this system. That this revolution was slower in takng place

James M. Zanutto
Hasselblad 500C, 1/250, f/8, Verichrome Pan film.

Charles Stern
*Hasselblad 1000F, 1/15, f/5.6,
Tri-X film.*

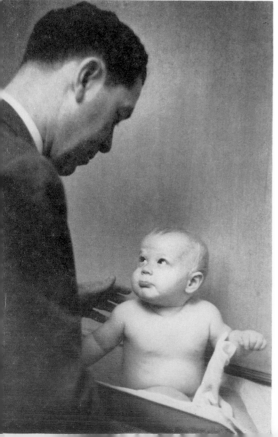

Murray Zinn
*Hasselblad 500C, 1/30, f/2.8,
Tri-X film.*

George Holton
Hasselblad 1000F, 60mm Distagon, 1 sec, f/11, Panatomic-X film.

among the larger cameras can, I should imagine, be attributed to the technological difficulties that had to be overcome.

For the working photographer, the SLR, exemplified in the 120-size field by the Hasselblad, has become an important working tool. The controls it gives him are tools which, if he uses them to the best advantage, will help him add a dimension of creativity to his photography.

SLR advantages

In close-ups, for instance, the twin-lens reflex photographer has, for some time, been able to make use of the Proxars and other close-up lens elements that shorten the focal length of his lens and allow him to advance within the 3- or 3½-ft limit that his normal lens requires him to maintain between camera and subject. But although closing in has allowed him to fill his

121

Ben McCall
Hasselblad 1000F, 1/50, f/11, Verichrome Pan film, with flash.

negative with a small image, it has given him, too, a problem of distortion to contend with. For the most part, and particularly in portraiture, he's found it more to his advantage not to close in, but instead to crop in the enlarging, in spite of the natural loss of quality inherent with this method. The Hasselblad, on the other hand, provides the usual Proxars for

Charles Stern
Hasselblad 1000F, 1/30, f/5.6, Tri-X film.

negative-filling, but offers the additional advantage of lens interchangeability, with the opportunity to use a telephoto lens for close-ups — filling
the negative without the distortion.

main or auxiliary camera

Fashion photographer Jules Alexander, for instance, owns a studio-view
camera as well as a 35mm camera, but his Hasselblad has become his

Ted Russell used a red filter and a three-second time exposure to make this remarkable silhouette of the New York skyline and the clouds above it.

studio's mainstay. He finds the view camera too slow for his efforts to capture spontaneity, and the 35mm camera often too small for the quality many of his advertising clients require. His Hasselblad works fast; his 150mm lens is probably the one he uses most, because he can fill a negative or a color transparency, while composing on the ground-glass screen to suit a client's layout or suggestion.

Dean Vincent, whose portraits of beautiful women have appeared in many magazines, uses a 135mm lens on a Hasselblad 1000F for his "first" camera.

On the other hand, George Holton, photographic illustrator, who averages a trip around the world just about every biennium, makes full

124

Hasselblad interchangeability dramatically illustrated here—front, back, top and side—lenses, magazines, film-advance knobs and viewing devices.

use of the compositional possibilities offered by his 60mm Distagon. In addition, he carries a Superwide, plus a normal and a telephoto lens. Holton's precisely arranged photographs — some of which appear in this book — usually require no cropping other than that planned when the image was still on the ground-glass screen, at which time he arranges for vertical or horizontal format. And very often, his final prints are square, representing the full negatives as they come from the tank.

Hasselblad advantages

Briefly, then, the basic Hasselblad SLR system offers these advantages — a combination not found on twin-lens reflex or rangefinder-type cameras:

(1) Full lens interchangeability — 60mm, 80mm, 150mm, and 250mm for the 500C; 60mm, 80mm, 135mm, and 250mm for the F-cameras.

(2) Interchangeable film magazines for all cameras (and interchangeable among the various models), with availability of a 16-exposure super-slide-size magazine, and a cut film adapter.

(3) Interchangeable viewing devices, with the availability of a critical-focusing magnifying viewer and accessory vewing frames for sportsfinders.

(4) On the 500C only, interchangeable film-advance knobs, with the availability of a knob with a built-in meter, a fast-winding crank, and, in the near future, an electric motor.

(5) Parallax-free operation.

(6) Selective focus and depth-of-field control.

(7) Bright ground-glass viewing and focusing.

(8) A full range of safety devices, and, finally, freedom from the danger of ever "taking a picture" without removing your lens cap.

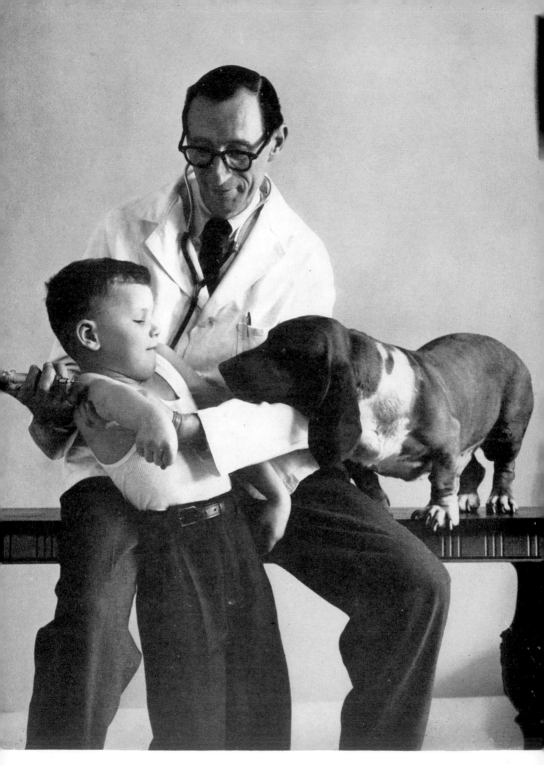

Jules Alexander

index